God and Coffee

IN THAT ORDER

God and Coffee

IN THAT ORDER

Kristina Seymour

ThomasMore®
– An RCL Company –
Allen, Texas

Send all inquiries to:
THOMAS MORE PUBLISHING
An RCL Company
200 East Bethany Drive
Allen, Texas 75002-3804

E-MAIL: WWW.RCLWEB.COM

BOOKSTORES:
CALL CHRISTIAN DISTRIBUTION SERVICES 888-444-2524
FAX 615-793-5973

INDIVIDUALS, PARISHES, AND SCHOOLS:
CALL THOMAS MORE PUBLISHING 800-822-6701
FAX 800-688-8356

INTERNATIONAL:
FAX THOMAS MORE PUBLISHING 972-264-3719

Printed in the United States of America

Library of Congress Catalog Number 00132147

ISBN 0-88347-450-6

1 2 3 4 5   04 03 02 01 00

CONTENTS

Preface

PREFACE

GOD AND COFFEE, IN THAT ORDER is a book about life's hectic schedule. It tells my story of God's faithfulness. It talks of moments when I sat on God's sandal and clung, as if a child to God's robe as he walked down roads I was too tired to walk myself. It tells of a time in my life when a full-time job as an assistant bookkeeper paid the bills, a job as a full-time English student at Georgia State University paved a road for my future, and it tells of a time when my two most important titles, motherhood and wife-hood, collided with the idea of sleep. This book does not just begin "Once upon a time," nor does it end "happily ever after." Somewhere between the beginning and end, though, there is a story. As you read the many stories and events of my days you will have the opportunity to read along with them the poem that was inspired by that story or event. Events in my life have steered me toward the Lord. I've cried out to the Lord in anguish, in joy, in pain, and in relief. The stories of my life are, I'm sure, much like your own; the poems written are God's words.

I've cried out to the Lord many times, but through it all I've always believed one thing. Laughter is almost as great as crying. Both events can bring tears to your eyes, but laughter is much more fun. Besides, it's the only thing you can do when you want to cry and someone is looking at you. And so when people ask how I do it all, I say, "God and coffee, in that order." For only with God could I stay up until 3:00 A.M. studying algebra and trigonometry after working all day and tiptoeing in to kiss my daughter goodnight. And only with God's strength and humor could I laugh at the coffee that spilled all over my homework because I fell asleep at 3:01 A.M. and knocked it over. *God and Coffee, In That Order* is a book about priorities and goals, about life and its struggles, but more importantly, it is a book about God's faithfulness.

❖

I PRAYED

A prayer can be such a relaxing event. I prayed one morning, as I usually do. I received the same warmth that God had always provided before. I received peace and loss of anxiety and a relief from stress. I received a hug, a moment of peaceful silence. I received a breath of fresh air as I stood tall and put my shoulders back, as if rearmed for another day. I received God's never-ending love. After my prayer I grabbed my coffee, grabbed my backpack, grabbed my purse, picked up my daughter, grabbed her diaper bag, grabbed my keys, forgot my lunch, grabbed a pen and wrote a quick "hi—bye" note to my husband, who I wouldn't see until he returned home from his day job as a student and his night job at Home Depot, then I headed out the door.

I reflected that night on my hectic day. I was thankful for God's strength and I told him so. I was thankful for his faithfulness and I thanked him for my daughter Faith. He listened as I reflected on my day, and he answered my prayer for strength and endurance as I needed to study and do well for another day. Every day I ask and every day he listens. And every day he answers my prayers for endurance. I laid my head back for a moment before I made a pot of coffee, and I prayed.

I Prayed ∾

I prayed a little this morning
As I drank my coffee.
I prayed for God's grace
To shower down on me.
I prayed I'd be strong and patient
As I faced my day
And that he'd trip the enemy
If he got in my way.
I prayed he would provide
For he always had before
And that I would listen
For that can be a chore.
And so I waited patiently and stood strong
While I listened
For God to give an answer,
My heart raced and then quickened.
And the earth did not tremble
Nor did lightning strike
But in my heart I saw a glimmer
Of God's gracious light.

BUT GOD HAS SURELY LISTENED AND
heard my voice in prayer.

PSALM 66:19

CHAPTER TWO

BOOT CAMP

I ran away from home at the age of eighteen. I was dating the man who would become my husband. I was enrolled in the local community college and the Grays Harbor County Beauty Pageant. I was living with my grandparents and life was not so bad. I ran away. I joined the air force. I have always been a practical person and I thought that even a silly task like running away should be handled responsibly. I left for San Antonio, Texas, on November 12 or so. This meant that I would spend all the holidays away from home, but I did not mind. I wanted to leave. I wanted out of "Dodge."

The interesting thing, though, is that I did not know what exactly I was doing, just that I was doing something. I guess, like the rest of the eighteen-year-olds there, I joined the military for college or, as the Sergeants said, to die for my country. I discovered who I was during training, but more importantly, as I faced the hideously funny experiences, as I faced fear as if I were in its alligator mouth, I discovered who God was. After my term in the air force, I learned something: Life is a boot camp. It's just as tough, even tougher. The walls are high and hard to scale. I balance my schedule and my roles as I once balanced upon a log. I'm tired and still envision sleeping on any cold slab of cement, no matter where it is. I want to cry and ask when it gets easier. Laughing, however, is more realistic. Besides, it raises less havoc on your eyelids. I compare my present life to boot camp at various times in my day, in my week, and in my life in general. I have realized a common occurrence . . . God was with me in the military's boot camp and he remains with me in the Boot Camp of Life.

BOOT CAMP ~

2:00 A.M. the bus pulled in

Their boots clicked upon the cement

Their Smokey Bear hats

Withstood the wind.

They roared like lions

Our eyes shook with fear

And then he was in my face

His breath hot and much too near.

Why are you here, little girl?

Did your mommy not want you?

Does the world?

Will you die for your country, will you sacrifice?

Are you tough as a tank and cold as ice?

Will you cry in the mud? When you scale the wall

Will you lead the cadence, or will you fall?

We made hospital corners, tight as a fist

They made us wiggle in our beds like worms

And said, What is this?

Make these beds again, do it some more

Next time it counts and we're keeping score

I balanced on a log seven feet high

I almost fell, then I looked to the sky

"God, please help me, don't let me fall

Help me run this race, help me scale the wall.

And quicker than light, I felt a hand

Upon my ribs, firmly I'd stand.

No one was around

For I was alone high

Above the ground—

But God was there he heard my cry

"When they shoot the M16 rounds," he said,

"To the ground tightly lay your head,

When they tease you, when they search your eyes

for tears

Have no fear

This is boot camp, BUT SO IS LIFE.

I'll show you why you are here, little girl

Your FATHER does want you in this world.

As words are fired like bullets to kill

As dark mud surrounds you

As fear attacks

Balance upon the log for

My hand is on your back!"

❖

IN THE DAY OF MY TROUBLE I WILL CALL
to you, for you will answer me.

PSALM 86:7

CHAPTER THREE

HAVE YOU?

I changed the sheets on our bed one weeknight. I had every intention of changing sheets that Sunday, but somehow between the grocery shopping, mopping, puppets with Faith, reading Emerson, reading Milton, writing a paper on Shakespeare, blocks with Faith, reading with Faith, and chasing Faith, it didn't get done. It may have been as far into the week as Wednesday when I finally changed the sheets; I don't remember for sure. I do remember the sound the sheets made when I shook them. A quick snap, shake, and a soft glide down to the bed as if an airborne trooper had just pulled his chute wide open. The sheet rested on the mattress and I quickly tucked and pulled, but I thought, "I'll write a poem tonight about sounds. About the sounds of sheets snapping, of strollers, of dogs barking, no, maybe not dogs, of basketballs bouncing . . . and I'll make it sound real." Why? "I don't know, it will come to me later," I thought. I continued with my chores. Faith brushed her teeth, we read ten Dr. Seuss stories, and around 10:00, I sat down on the couch with a cup of coffee, a pen, and a piece of paper, and I wrote.

HAVE YOU? ∼

Have you listened to crisp sheets
As you shake them during chores?
Have you heard a lion
As he roars?
Have you heard crickets
In a deep southern sky?
Have you heard a child
Sweetly ask, "But why?"
Have you heard a train
Far far away?
Have you heard a bird
In the morning or the day?
Have you heard a stroller's wheels
As a father and child walk by?
Have you heard the flaps
Of the wings of a firefly?
Have you heard a basketball
Dribbled in a gym?
Have you heard God's voice?
Have you prayed to him?

❀

Sᴇᴇ ᴛᴏ ɪᴛ ᴛʜᴀᴛ ʏᴏᴜ ᴅᴏ ɴᴏᴛ ʀᴇꜰᴜꜱᴇ ʜɪᴍ
who speaks. If they did not escape when they
refused him who warned them on earth, how
much less will we, if we turn away from him
who warns us from heaven?

HEBREWS 12:25

CHAPTER FOUR

I KNOW

I was sitting across from a good friend in a Mexican restaurant telling her the story of my life in a nutshell. Through the course of the meal and the course of my stories, I mentioned several times what God had "said" to me at different times in my life. The whole concept of God saying things and the fact that he exists was a little new to her and she said, "It seems God has said (and she emphasized this word) many things to you. How did he say these things? What? Did you hear a real voice say these things to you?" She caught me off guard because I simply had heard God speak to me and I did not know how to explain his voice to someone who had not ever heard it.

I mentioned my dilemma and my inability to handle the situation to a Christian friend and she told me how to handle it in the future. My Christian friend told me that next time the subject comes up to tell the "questioning individual" to ask God to speak to her heart in such a way that she would know that he was speaking. She told me to pray that God would speak to her in some way, through some action, somehow in his own way that only God and the "questioning individual" would understand. "That's all you need to do," she said. "If you ask God to speak to someone he will." She said that I can be sure that God will speak to their heart and I can be sure that they will know it is God speaking. "God hears us when we ask for things," she said. "And you can be sure he will speak to those trying to listen."

I KNOW ～

I know I have brown hair
I know my eyes are blue.
I know I'll get ready for work tomorrow
I know the size of my shoe.
I know my birthday
I know your birthday, too.
I know what a cow says,
Simply, always, "Moo."
I know God's voice
As simply as all these things
But his voice is nothing of this earth
For he is the King of kings.
His voice is powerful
His voice is point-blank
His voice can rescue
A ship even if it has sank.
His voice is obvious
To those who seek him out
His voice is so clear that he whispers
As if a shout.
His voice is just his voice
It cannot be explained.
And your heart will know his voice
Just as your eyes know a flame.

MY DEAR BROTHERS, TAKE NOTE OF THIS:
Everyone should be quick to listen, slow to
speak and slow to become angry.

JAMES 1:19

TODAY, IF YOU HEAR HIS VOICE, DO NOT
harden your hearts as you did in the rebellion.

HEBREWS 3:15

CHAPTER FIVE

DEAR CHILD

Every night Faith and I pray. She's only two and a half, but she's thankful for her bottle of milk, her toes, her daddy, her baby dolls, her pillow, her eyebrows, her grandma Joy, her Becky (her aunt), her Mel (her other aunt), her Holly Dog (her grandma Joy's dog), her grandma Val, and her new boots her grandma Val bought at a garage sale. She folds her hands and says "Amen Jesus!" In hopes of teaching her at a young age to thank God for all she has, in hopes that she'll come to know Jesus before the world tells her not to, we pray. I pray when she's done and she lays quietly and listens. I pray for her strength and endurance, that she'll listen and follow God all the days of her life, that she won't fall so far from his reach that she doesn't know he's there. I pray that her life brings glory to his name and that she touches others with his love. I pray with all my soul that she will marry a godly man who loves God first and her entirely. This I pray every night. With tears in my eyes I wrote a poem one night to that effect. I wrote "Dear Child" so that Faith will always remember my love, my prayer, and God's love for her.

I know that many parents everywhere pray for their children. But may God knock louder than a fire engine on the hearts of parents who have yet to discover God and prayer and may every child in the world have someone say "Dear Child."

DEAR CHILD ～

Dear child

You are beautiful

For your not so carefully chosen words

For you repeat what you see

And all of what you've heard.

And may I please remind you

Of the beauty you possess

Your deep dark eyes

Your soft strong hands

You are so very wise.

You've taught me more

Than Shakespeare, Milton, Dante,

Or Ralph Waldo—

You've taught me how to live

And love, and how to let go.

May I teach you how to love

Yourself—love God deep and true

For he will guide your path

In this life he's given you.

Don't stray, don't hesitate

Don't listen to those who lie

And ground yourself in the Word

And you'll never ask, For why?

For why this? Or for why that?

Why am I here?

Dear child, these questions

From your heart

Should not be near.

Pray and find answers,

Ask, you will receive

The will of God, thus your will,

In your heart believe.

Believe you are beautiful

Believe you are strong

Believe you are powerful

Sing yourself this song.

May I give you

Character, confidence in yourself

Faith in God.

Thus, this is your name

Thus pray, listen, hear, and nod.

For life will be hard

God never promised it would be easy.

Heroes should be parents

Thus, I pray one you see in me.

May I be a model

May I be your friend

May you always feel

My heart and ear I'll lend.

Stand fast as if a warrior

Majestic in the wind

May the flag you hold ripple

As your many journeys end and begin again.

Stand fast! Stand fast!

Battle the storms

Fight for what is right!

This I pray for you

This prayer I pray ev'ry night.

❖

Train a child in the way he should go, and when he is old he will not depart from it.

PROVERBS 22:6

CHAPTER SIX

No Title

After Spanish 103 around 9:00 A.M. I jotted across campus to the library. My goal was to sign in at the computer lab and get an extra credit point while working on a Spanish study lesson. My professor, Delgado Jenkins, allowed us to earn up to six extra credit points that would go toward our final grade. Not wanting to miss the opportunity, for I was not exactly fluent in Española, I signed in, found a computer, and sat down. I had an hour before my next class and I was ready to *estudiar* (study). Almost without thought, I did not pull up the Spanish lesson. I double-clicked into Word Perfect and I wrote a poem.

My first class was at 8:00 A.M. and since I worked until 8:00 P.M. or 9:00 P.M. and since I tried to spend at least ten minutes with my daughter before she went to sleep, and since I still had homework to do at 11:00 P.M., I did not get much sleep. Maybe I slept four hours, sometimes three hours, and if a paper was due or a test or quiz was scheduled, none. I did not procrastinate. I simply did not have enough time in a day to get it all done. This poem does not have a title, simply because I wrote it without thought, but it was inspired by the stress and pressure of my day. The wonderful thing, though, is that I wrote it based on exhaustion, but I ended within God's strength.

No Title ∾

The world all encompassing surrounds me

And I stretch and notice birds and sky.

Challenges exist as if a serpent

That searches for those who wish to die.

My eyes glisten as if a crystal lake

For tears wish to come

But I have much more to accomplish

Before this life of mine is done.

The winds run as if a race

And the leaves battle for a rest

And I too desire a place

For deep contemplation at its best.

For my challenge is large and

Thinks he's stronger than I

But God is my weapon, my victorious shield

He gives me my strength, my wings appear,

And I begin to fly.

❖

But THOSE WHO HOPE IN THE LORD WILL renew their strength. They will soar on wings like eagles; they will run and not grow weary, they will walk and not be faint.

ISAIAH 40:31

CHAPTER SEVEN

THE BOXING RING

Boxing is a brutal sport. It's physically exhausting. It's one man against another. It's about challenge and it revolves around adrenaline. For the man in America who does not end up in a boxing ring, for the man who is busy and working but loves the thrill of it all; for this man there is a garage, a punching bag, and gloves of his own. The deep-padded thud and force of a glove devouring the bag is satisfying to this man. The sweat that drips off his brow stings his eye, maybe, but he continues. For it's a victorious ever-exhausting wonderful thing to throw punches and sweat and exhaust one's day, one's pain, upon the bag.

I wrote "The Boxing Ring" because my husband has a garage, a punching bag, and gloves of his own. My husband taught me about the demand of boxing and about the thrill and accomplishment of it all. My husband faces challenges in his life, within his mind, and within his garage. Although we all may not box, we all are stubborn to some extent, and because we all struggle to rid ourselves of pain, of loss, of tears, and of sweat. I wrote "The Boxing Ring" because life is challenging and if we let down our guard, the blows will come and knock us out, *because we all need God.*

THE BOXING RING 〜

The boxing ring
Had no mercy.
The rails were hard rubber
The floor disgustingly hard
The opponent mean as a bull
My heart ached and outward it pulled.
The shin splints within my legs
Seemed to scream out loud
As if to say,
"This ring exists to torture the soul
of anyone who tries to conquer
the opponent's throws."
And so if you dare to take the challenge

And dance and swing punches

While sweat drips off your brow

Go ahead, but "the Ring of Life"

Is stronger somehow.

So unless you have God as your agent

Stay in your garage and box

Where you'll be safe (for now)

But forever stagnant.

FINALLY, BE STRONG IN THE LORD AND IN his mighty power. Put on the full armor of God so that you can take your stand against the devil's schemes.

EPHESIANS 6:10-11

CHAPTER EIGHT

GOD'S SUNFLOWER

I have a best friend who loved me when times were tough, when I was rough around the edges, when I was angry, and when I was sad. She loved me when I was funny, too, but more importantly, when I was in pain. We ran into each other at the local mall a couple days after we had graduated from high school. We met two boys who incidentally became fine men and who also became our husbands. That is a story in itself. Brenda is her name, she married Grant (the other man at the phone booth), and I married Brian. We've been best friends ever since. I left for the military, she left for California. Brian and Grant were Airborne Rangers in the army and they jumped out of planes and discovered the exciting thrills of life while we went off to discover ourselves.

One of the greatest times in my life was the summer before I left for the air force. The year was 1991. Brenda and I met "the guys" and our lives have not been the same since. We all went on picnics, we went to parks, we went to movies, we went to dinner, we talked for hours, we laughed, we were carefree. Brian and I live in Georgia now. Brenda and Grant live in Washington. He's a deputy, she's an insurance agent. Brian and I are raising Faith and going to school. Times have changed, miles have come between us, but the Lord remains within our hearts and within our friendship. I thank God for her all the time. I call her and she always tells me something I need to hear. She clarifies a conflict, she takes away tears, she talks of God and all his power, and I love her so much.

Brenda is a tall, beautiful blonde. She came over once before Brian and I moved away. Brenda and I ran to the store to get more flavored creamer for our coffee (she loves coffee too) and we walked into the grocery store together. Now, I'm a wonderfully cute brunette, five-foot-five, freckles, blue eyes, fair skin (I think God was going to make me a redhead and then at the last minute said, "No, let's do something unique with her"). Oh, and let's not forget my wonderful smile. So now that you have a picture in your mind of me, let us discuss Brenda's looks. She's gorgeous, "could be a model" gorgeous. Tall, thin, tan (even though she lives in Washington State!), white smile, hazel eyes, and she has a great personality. She's a cover girl. Anyway, we walked into the store and, I'm not joking, a man ran into a loud-noise-making bunch of stuff with his cart! One would think that only happens in the movies, but not everyone has a best friend as beautiful as Brenda. One of the many great things about Brenda, though, is that she is as beautiful on the inside as she is on the outside. It's been two years since I've seen her. I miss her and I sent her this poem.

GOD'S SUNFLOWER ～

I looked for a sunflower

In the perfect shade

To brighten

Up your day.

I could not find

The one I desired

So I bought an orange

Tulip that was warm as fire.

I looked for a perfect rose

One that was cream

With the essence of gold.

I wanted something

Full of grace for your hand

That would sound the trumpets

In heaven's band.

So far away, though, so I prayed

That God would place a sunflower

Along your path today.

ALL MEN ARE LIKE GRASS, AND ALL THEIR glory is like the flowers of the field; the grass withers and the flowers fall, but the word of the Lord stands forever.

I PETER 1:24-25

CHAPTER NINE

DETERMINATION

I was raised by my mother with the help of my grandparents. My parents divorced when I was one or so and I hardly remember my father. He has since passed away. I never knew him nor do I know if he knew the Lord. My mother was working hard as a waitress to support me and my two brothers. I began praying at an early age though I never understood it. My two brothers, my cousin, and I were dropped off at church on Easter; my mom, stepfather, or aunt never came inside. I didn't know who God was. I only knew of him as a concept or something that other kids had. I grew up quickly. I blinked and my childhood was gone. It seemed I had too many people to take care of, or so I thought I should. I thank God for my mom and my grandparents who taught me about responsibility and respect and about hard work. I thank God for at least a small amount of order in my world of chaos. And I say all this, not because I am sad, not because I want to be on Oprah, but because it's fact and it's my history.

I thank God that I learned at an early age that life is what you make it. And I thank God for teaching me that without him you can't make it at life. Because of my past and my struggles, I am very determined. I don't stop. I don't quit; I refuse to. A friend once told me what an acquaintance said about me. She said, "Kristina is like the racehorse that you know you can bet

on, you know she's gonna win, you know she's gonna make it."
I appreciated the comment. It's nice to know that other people
recognize my determination. It's important that people also see
that my determination is God-given and God-driven. Whatever
I say I will do, I do. Not to say that I get whatever I want when
I want it, but I believe through Christ all things are possible.
Since God moved mountains and parted the Red Sea, I know
that he can help me accomplish his goals. Many people pat me
on the back and admire my determination. Many people refuse
to acknowledge God's strength within my life and within my
accomplishments. In response to these pats on my back I wrote
"Determination."

DETERMINATION ~

I reach for a goal

I achieve it every time

For though he giveth me the strength

And through me he shines

Most act amazed

At my abilities

And I just respond

Only by his mercy.

"No," they say, as Satan whispers in their ear,

"It's by your strength, it's just your way."

And Satan quietly disappears.

I argue and say,

"I alone cannot accomplish all I do in a day.

Only through prayer and by his grace."

Again, I do say

They do not listen and

They applaud my determination

But I repeat, "I walk

In the imprint of their feet

That help me in my hesitation,

For I am just a child

Of thy Father

Of creation."

I PRESS ON TOWARD THE GOAL TO WIN THE prize for which God has called me heavenward in Christ Jesus.

PHILIPPIANS 3:14

CHAPTER TEN

Pro-Life

I pray that God have mercy on a nation that kills its unborn children. A nation's ability to do this can be traced back to its love of money, greed, hunger for power—for control, and lack of morals. In simple terms, it is the result of a country lacking God. I believe that the huge lack of respect that seems to have plagued this country can be traced back to its ability to kill an unborn child. I feel so strongly about this injustice that my heart aches, my stomach knots, and I write. I wrote "Pro-Life" in an attempt to capture the essence of peace within the womb. I reached into the inner depths of my soul searching for words that would paint a picture upon your eyelids of a country, a tiger, that kills a child. I pray that "Pro-Life" inspires others to take a stand and fight for the life of the unborn child.

Pro-Life ∼

Within an all-encompassing warm luminescent light
Exists a place full of love and emotions that
Run bright

Mingled laughter, motions of praise.

Surrounded by softness greater than the fur of a tiger
And though the softness is more magnificent than
The anger of the tiger's eyes,

Softly, I hide.

May I always be surrounded by these walls
Of protection

This, my house, my life is mine to dance and mingle
With people

And sip the Lord's wine.

And may I break the bread and fold my hands
In prayer

And may I learn and teach and inspire

And may I not hear the voice of a liar.

FOR I EXIST, I AM HERE! And may my words nestle
In your heart

And awaken your soul

To others that insist that I leave and say I must go.

For I know outside this house of mine is a jungle,
A land,

Full of love that will someday take a stand.

And may the small hum of peace and the beat of
MY LIFE that I hear

Continue to dance with the moonlight that I
See sometimes.

And may the murmuring sounds that connect me
To you

Protect me from the tiger

And his eyes of anger.

May I not meet the tiger who longs for my life

But may I only feel his fur's softness in roles as a mother and a wife

Or for others, who Could grow to be men of God

May they Not meet the tiger and his paws of steel and sod.

For the tiger is there, filthy and wild

But I am here; warm . . . I will be safe

FOR I AM JUST A CHILD.

❖

IT WAS HE WHO GAVE SOME TO BE apostles, some to be prophets, some to be evangelists, and some to be pastors and teachers, to prepare God's people for works of service, so that the body of Christ may be built up until we all reach unity in the faith and in the knowledge of the Son of God and become mature, attaining to the whole measure of fullness of Christ. Then we will no longer be infants, tossed back and forth by the waves, and blown here and there by every wind of teaching and by cunning and craftiness of men in their deceitful scheming. Instead, speaking the truth in love, we will in all things grow up into him who is Head, that is, Christ. From him the whole body, joined and held together by every supporting ligament grows and builds itself up in love, as each part does its work.

EPHESIANS 4: 11-16

CHAPTER ELEVEN

A MAGICIAN

I was at work even after the "quitting time" whistle in my assembly-line mind had rung, and I was talking to a wonderful secretary friend. She's much older than I; well, she's not much older—maybe twelve years or so, but I think of her as wise. She always tells me something funny in a comedian kind of way. Or she tells me something very inspiring and deep. I like her for her experiences, her tough childhood, and for her ability to overcome all those things and still be a pleasant person. She says she's going to write a book one day. If she ever does I will tell all I know to buy it for I know it will be as wonderful as all the "quitting-time conversations" I've had with her. She told me that she read somewhere or someone said (she wasn't sure exactly where she discovered it), "To be a good writer and to write well, one has to put something in the hat before they can pull something out." True, true, *true!*

I began to write frantically in my head on the way home while sitting in bumper-to-bumper Atlanta traffic. If Atlanta traffic is good for anything, it's an automatic sit-down-and-take-a-break moment of the day because you simply can't move, you can't run, you can't stop doing homework to clean the messy house, and you can't pay bills: you just have to sit. In a way I've come to enjoy mentally writing in the car. My friend inspired me. She was so right. For only now that I'm exhausted and full of life changes and experiences do I write passionately and with all my heart. Because only now can I relate to the world. I've been there now. I've had a rough childhood, dealt with the alcoholism of a loved one (and come to understand what it's all about), I've been in the military and I've shot an M16, while all the time wanting (but never acting on that desire) to scream like Private Benjamin and ask where the condos are, I've given birth!, I've moved cross-country, I've lived with in-laws while our mortgage loan came through (no offense, Joy, it was just a crowded wait: love ya), I've had hideous jobs and dreadful bosses. Now I can say I've been there, I've felt like that, I'm there, and I'm trying to go there. I've learned to trust God and I love to write about it all. And so I wrote this poem around 5:39 P.M., while sitting in bumper-to-bumper traffic, while smiling at the realization that it is true, you do have to "put something in the hat before you can pull something out."

A Magician ∿

As if out of a magic hat

flow the words

then God whispers, "Is this what needs

to be heard?"

I stop, I wait,

I contemplate

and begin again.

As if many ribbons at Christmas-time

were curled round and round

and as if they softly fell

from the sky to the ground:

I write where I've been, what I see,

what I hear

God seems to make words ice-skate gracefully

as a message becomes clear.

The rabbit hopped away

long since gone to a field

and words exist now deep within the hat

emerging solid as if a shield.

The pain I've known

was to understand—

the magician's audience claps as a pink, orange,

blue, purple then white

handkerchief emerges from my hand.

THOUGH YOU HAVE NOT SEEN HIM, YOU
love him; and even though you do not see him
now, you believe in him and are filled with an
inexpressible and glorious joy.

I PETER 1: 8

CHAPTER TWELVE

A Walk

I went on a walk with Faith the other day. We were going to collect treasures. Treasures are such things as rocks, leaves, lost pennies, acorns, and whatever else happens to look interesting. We brought her pink Barbie purse and her baby buggy full of Mickey Mouse, three baby dolls, and a few Beanie Babies. We were ready to tackle the neighborhood. I let Faith lead the way. She wanted to sit on a patch of the neighbor's lawn on the curb, so we did. We discovered that a huge red and black ant was carrying another ant in his clenching jaws! We took advantage of this Discovery Channel moment to watch. We discussed the possibility that the big ant was helping the other ant, but then we decided that he was going to kill him! We quickly knocked the helpless ant loose of the monstrous ant's clenching teeth! It felt great to know we were heroes! The monster ant ran in circles double-checking his hunting territory. He circled about five times and then scampered up a leaf and stuck out his antennas trying to figure out what on earth had happened. Eventually, he went back into the grass and we decided that we should be collecting treasures anyway.

I saw the world through a child's eyes on that walk. I smelled the air and the grass, and listened to the leaves. Faith reminded me of the wonderful viewpoint a child has upon the world. Somehow adult life, mortgages, bills, and goals get in the way of drawing in dirt and picking grass, piling up leaves and then jumping in them. When we returned from our walk Faith yelled, "Mark, get set, *go!*" as she ran up the hill in our front yard. I decided that it was time that I took my marks, got set, and slowed down. After all, there might be some bigger treasures I've been missing out on.

A WALK ～

I took a walk one day

with the best guide in town

for my little girl was always happy

and her little voice, the sweetest sound.

We discovered many treasures

rocks, leaves, acorns and such

and somehow deep inside

my heart was reminded of God's touch.

For if I let God be the leader

on every walk I took

the treasures found if listed

would overflow a book.

I bet God would splash in puddles and leap from

rock to rock

I bet God would climb the grandest tree

and sail a toy boat down the creek as if it never

knew a dock.

I bet God would laugh and tell jokes

funny enough to tickle my toes.

I bet on a walk with God
the fun would overflow.
I bet if I ran real fast and fell
and skinned my knee
God would pick me up and say,
"It's okay, follow me."
I bet God has invited me to take
many walks with him
I bet God whispered in my ear
through that leaf out on the limb.
I bet God was there the other day
when I took a walk with my child
to remind me of the simple things
that are more worthwhile.
I think I'll stop for now on
to accept ants and broken leaves
as wonderful treasures
worth more than what they seem.

WHEN I WAS A CHILD, I TALKED LIKE A child, I thought like a child. I reasoned like a child. When I became a man, I put childish ways behind me. Now we see but a poor reflection as in a mirror; then we shall see face to face. Now I know in part; then I shall know fully, even as I am fully known.

I CORINTHIANS 13:11-12

CHAPTER THIRTEEN

LOST

My cousin is one month older than I. We grew up together playing Barbie dolls and eating peanut butter and jelly sandwiches, dunking them in milk while sitting on a curb. We made up games, we stayed up late, we slept outside in the summer. We were more like sisters and I love her so much. The wonderful thing about God is that he does not force us to love him. He gives us choices and sometimes we do not make the right ones. I wish I could force God's love on people that I love. I wish I could demand that they not have a choice and that they love Jesus. I can't, though. My cousin was lost somewhere between the ages of twelve and twenty-four. Drugs, violence, jail, depression, and confusion seem to have invaded her heart. I pray that God invades her heart. If she reads this book I pray that she remembers the wonderful days of our youth and that we are all children of God; no matter where we've been.

LOST ~

I found a lost puppy

I hung up signs everywhere

"Lost puppy, white and black,

call this number if you care."

I found a lost doll at the park

the little girl who left her had long since gone.

I found a lost coat in the mall

inside the tag read Seymour, John.

I found a lost tennis ball

by the tennis court in the thicket

there I also saw a lost kitten

and a cricket.

All of this I saw one summer when I was young

but now that I am older

my "Lost and Found" list has just begun.

Lost people, confused souls scared

and all alone

as if they were a kite next to mountains

dangerously blown.

I call out, I try, I yell

I must be heard

"You are more important than lost kittens,

coats, crickets,

and even birds."

Please walk up to the counter

down the hall on your right

God is there to erase you from the lost list

He understands your plight.

For you are receiving the goal of your faith, the salvation of your souls.

I PETER 1:9

CHAPTER FOURTEEN

THE LESSON

As a child I was not taught about Jesus. Easter was because of the Easter Bunny, Christmas was about giving presents. I really felt the void in my heart when I entered my teen years and started questioning myself and my life. I heard about Jesus, I went to church with friends, and, of course, I realized what the Christian holidays meant. I knew a girl in high school who everyone knew was from a "holy roller" family. It seemed she had a bad rap because everyone knew she was full of God and all his rigidness. I have since realized that none of this was true. If anything was true it was that she seemed to be armed with God and all his strength. She did not fall into peer pressure the way most of us did. She did not question things that would bring her harm. She was stronger than I was, she had something I did not. She had Jesus. I know for a fact that my teen years would not have been so traumatic had I known who she knew. God is referred to as a rock. He is a God of salvation and of undefeated strength. I almost slipped through the cracks during my teen years. I had everything going for me, but I felt lost. I did not know if I was coming or going, or where I was supposed to be going, for that matter. This girl I knew faced the same situations that I did, the same peer pressure, the same inner struggles, but she was grounded on the rock.

Teaching our children about Jesus is more important than manners, bedtime stories, cleanliness, and respect. Jesus is the one thing we can teach them that can change their lives and save them. Manners may get our children appraisal from other parents, respect may get them an interview later in life, but Jesus is the one thing we can teach them about and at the same time save their lives.

Faith is a little over two. The other day we were talking about Christmas and she said, "Jesus' birthday." She skinned her knee and she said, "It's okay. Jesus will fix it." I'm proud to know that she knows Jesus and I'm thankful already for the support that he will give her during her teen years and beyond.

THE LESSON ∼

Brush your teeth, pick a story, but first

say your prayer

thank God for your milk

and cast away your cares.

"Thank you, dear Lord," I say,

and Faith sweetly adds,

"for my Barney, my toes,

and my dad.

Love Grandmom Val, Grandmom Joy,

and Jesus too, luv you."

"Thank you, Jesus, for all you do,"

I chime in.

"May Faith always choose you above sin."
Faith will know you later in life
when she feels all alone
Her two-year-old heart will remind her
of the butterfly wings you made
that she saw flown.
When she has children
she'll say, "Brush your teeth and say your prayer"
and she'll think she's become her mother!
and wonder how and where
it happened.

YOU ARE ALL SONS OF GOD THROUGH
faith in Christ Jesus, for all of you who were
baptized into Christ have clothed yourself
with Christ.

GALATIANS 3:26

CHAPTER FIFTEEN

JESUS LIVES

My grandpaw was a wonderful man. If you noticed, I spelled grandpa with a "w" on the end. He always said my hands were so plump and cute as a child that they looked like St. Bernard paws. I might add that although I have grown up, my hands still look like St. Bernard paws. Regardless, my grandpaw had a "w" on the end of his name. Harry Arthur Hamilton grew up in Thorpe, Washington. He did not have a nice stepfather. In fact, his stepfather was so mean to him I don't like to think about it. My grandpaw never went to college, but he was a brilliant man. Grandpaw told me numerous times of the opportunity he had to live with his high school football coach after graduating from high school and attending college. The college thing never happened for grandpaw, though. I don't know all the facts, but it was something about how grandpaw had to "work the farm."

I never knew my father. My parents divorced when I was only a year old. I had one most horrific stepfather for fourteen years of my life. About the time the third stepfather was about to assume his role in my life, I moved out of my mother's house and moved in with my grandparents. During the first fourteen years of my life, I as well as my mother, my two brothers, and the first step-father lived on and off with my grandparents in their basement. I think my two brothers and I were the only ones in the world who slept in a three-story bunk bed sky-scraper, built by a stepfather who, after he received his building permit for "this major bunk bed bidding," never lifted another finger in his life. I guess all these details could start a whole book of their own, but I won't "go there" right now. The simple truth is that because of my unique family situation I "lived" with my grandparents most of my life anyway, so moving in with them "officially" at the age of fifteen was not a big adjust-ment. I always considered my grandpaw to be my dad. He coached my softball teams, he drove me to my state soccer tour-naments, he went to my track meets, he taught me how to drive, he loaned me $1,200 to buy my first car because he knew I would pay it back quickly (and when I did he bragged on the fact for years afterward to all the relatives and family friends), and he helped me with my math homework. The fact that he helped me with my math homework was a heroic act in itself. He used to get so frustrated when he would go to great lengths to explain a math problem while I quietly looked like I under-stood, only to hear me say, "I don't get it?!"

He was my dad in every sense of the word. He and I were very close. Grandpaw was not a Christian during my childhood years, but he was a very fine man. He was a broad-shouldered, strong-looking, sturdy, stout man, and he spoke in a voice that commanded one to listen. He did not say much, but, boy, when he did talk, you had better listen. He expected that we knew to respect him because he was Grandpaw. If you were sitting in his chair when he walked in the living room, you'd better jump up, even though he said to me a hundred times, "No, don't move." The fact that I always voluntarily got up out of his chair, the fact that when he let me borrow his car, I filled it up, moved the seat back to where *he* had it, and the fact that I put the keys in the same left hand I got them out of, was a result of our special rela-tionship. I remember borrowing a fifteen-cent stamp from him when I was a kid and he said, "You can give me back fifteen cents or you can give me back a stamp, but make sure you give me back one or the other." He ripped paper towels in half because he lived during the depression and because those huge things were really a waste for just one person. I respected him because to me he was the greatest man who ever lived. He was always there for me. He respected me because he knew I was "a good kid."

When I became a Christian I battled with mustering up enough courage to "talk" to Grandpaw about God. I couldn't imagine Grandpaw would react angrily and shoot me down or say "shut up," but the mere thought of approaching Grandpaw with such subject matter scared the pants off me! I joined the military, left for training, got married, and had a child before I even starting growing enough hair on my chest to fathom the idea. I prayed for a good year for the perfect opportunity to talk to Grandpaw. The time just never seemed right, or I just seemed too scared. Well, it was September of 1995 when my husband and I traveled the hour to Montesano, Washington (we lived in Olympia), to say goodbye to everyone before we packed up the U-Haul and drove cross-country to Georgia to finish college and begin our new lives. I knew it was the last time I'd see Grandpaw and I knew I needed to talk to him no matter how stupid or scared I felt. A bunch of us were outside in the driveway. Some were shooting hoops, others were talking on the lawn, and some people were back and forth between outside and the kitchen. Somehow or another Grandpaw and I were separated from the others and I was sitting on the hood of my car and Grandpaw was leaning on my car and we were just talking. I just blurted out, "Grandpaw, did you ever go to church as a child? Or did your mom not teach you about Jesus?" He said that his mother used to give him two pennies and send him off to church by himself. "Of course," he said, "when I got back Mother would ask me about church and wondered how I ended up with so much candy for the price of *one* penny. I told her that I was walking along and I dropped Jesus' penny for church, but mine I still had, so I spent *mine* on candy." That was Grandpaw's way of saying, yes, he was told of Jesus, but somehow he never really saw Jesus in the way his mother lived or the fact that she was married to such an awful man. It was Grandpaw's way of saying, "I know people have said he's alive, but I've never found it out or seen him for myself." Grandpaw said he couldn't really imagine a heaven with a bunch of pretty maidens dancing around nor could he really imagine a hell with fire and a pitch fork. I told him that there was a heaven and hell and that Jesus did live and that all you had to do was believe in Jesus to know him. We were interrupted at this point because someone wanted to get a group picture or something. When Brian and I left that day, my heart was broken and tears ran down my face all the way home. Grandpaw had followed our car all the way down the driveway and then he continued to walk on the gravel part of the road. As we drove out of sight I saw Grandpaw standing by his mailbox looking at me look at him. I remember telling Brian that I had finally said something to Grandpaw about Jesus, but I wasn't sure it was enough and I really hoped it was because I knew Grandpaw was going to die soon and I wanted him to be with Jesus.

Two weeks after we had been in Georgia I called my sister-in-law and the first thing she said was, "Kristina, it's your grandpaw, he had a heart attack and they are working on him *right now!*" I said, "He's gone." She said, "You don't know that, they are working on him as we speak and they might be able to . . ." "He's gone," I said, "and it's all right." I knew the instant my grandpaw left this world. I could not tell you the time he died, but I can tell you I knew the instant he died because I had the most overwhelming sense of peace. I felt lifted off the couch. I knew Grandpaw was with Jesus and I was so happy for him that it overshadowed the fact that his earthly body was gone. I felt the most warm, comforting, uplifting sense of peace and I knew Grandpaw was in heaven. I cried for days and I was so very sad that my heart ached because the death of a loved one does that to the ones who are left behind, but Grandpaw is with Jesus and even when I cry and miss him terribly, I just thank God that the most wonderful man I ever knew received Jesus in his heart before he died. I'm so thankful.

JESUS LIVES ～

Jesus is alive

He lives

I know he's there

I see him in others

The way they love and care.

Jesus exists, though you've never seen him shake

An umbrella after the rain

Or in a suit dressed to a "T"

Handing out business cards with his name.

He's not working here as a hot dog vendor

In New York

He's not posing as a waiter

Arranging knives and forks.

He's not undercover as an ordinary Joe

Mingling with the locals

Nonchalantly telling everyone

How to live, what to do, and where to go.

He lives in the hearts of the umbrella shaker,

"the suit man," the vendor, the waiter, and me.

It is through one's eyes of faith

That makes Jesus so simple to see.

---❖---

For WHAT I RECEIVED I PASSED ON TO YOU as of first importance: that Christ died for our sins according to the Scriptures, that he was buried, that he was raised on the third day according to the Scriptures.

I CORINTHIANS 15:3-4

CHAPTER SIXTEEN

PACKED HEARTS

Think back to your childhood lunch. Your lunch as a child says a lot about your childhood. I remember some of the kids had the greatest lunches. They had a kind of sandwich other than peanut butter and jelly. They had anything ranging from sliced apples, mozzarella string cheese, individual-sized bags of chips (Doritos, Cheetos, corn chips were the ultimate), they had the awesome flavor of Capri Sun for their drink, Oreo cookies (not the generic), they may have even had Velveeta singles. A lunch with just two of these items was an amazing lunch to have. I never had all that expensive stuff, but my mom always wrote "Have a nice day" on my napkin. My mom always tried to make up for the fact that we didn't have a lot of money and the fact that our stepfather was hideous. As a silly child I thought that if I just had those Velveeta (that real expensive cheese) slices or a Capri Sun in my lunch then I would be just like the other kids who had a nice (real) dad, and a quiet place to sit and do homework, then and maybe then I would be "just a normal kid with normal kid problems." Looking back, it's funny that I thought if my lunch was different then my life would be different as well.

I knew when I grew up I would keep that expensive Velveeta cheese in the fridge. I knew I would get up early enough to pack my own children's lunches. "They are going to have Capri Suns,

Doritos, string cheese, a ham sandwich with time-consuming lettuce, and a fancy tomato, and a 'Have a nice day' napkin." I planned on giving my kids everything and I decided that since a nice lunch and a nice napkin would make my children's day, then it would be my responsibility as a mom to provide *both* things for them. Now that I'm grown and I have my own children, now that I'm mature enough to look back at my "lunch theory," I realize the importance of much more than a fancy lunch. It's pretty simple, really. It's my job as a parent to provide a quiet, non-fighting, non-alcoholic environment in which my children can do homework. It's my job as a parent to make my children feel as special as God made them. It's my job as a parent to realize that the small things like "what's in their lunch" can translate into something rather huge in their little minds. My children will not long to be "just a normal kid with normal kid problems." They will be the kids with the "Have a nice day" napkins. They will more than likely hide the napkin note real quick in order to save themselves from utter humiliation because they have a "corny" mom. They may have generic cookies, but they'll have a box of juice. They may not have tomatoes and lettuce for their sandwiches, but they'll have one or the other.

Reality check: Let's face it, a child does not need ten expensive items in their lunch bag to make them feel special. It's also not realistic to try to cut and chop and bag and pack a real fancy lunch at 6:00 A.M. before the bus comes. It is realistic to pack a lunch with love and write something nice on their napkin. It is realistic to set standards for one's household and to not accept anything other than a sober, loving environment.

I believe God has a "Pack Their Bags Theory" that puts my lunch theory to shame. You see, God has his own ideas of what children need packed in their bags. In his version, their bags are really *their hearts*. He wants their hearts full of "expensive Velveeta cheese." Of course, his idea of expensive cheese is really *expensive time*. He wants us to spend precious time with them no matter what the cost. No matter if we have to rearrange our work schedules (our college schedules) in order to be home with them and do two puzzles before dinner. No matter if we have to stop what we're doing in order to listen to what they want to do, i.e., "play." Time is expensive. It is precious. He wants us to spend, spend, and then spend some more time with our kids. God's idea of a "fancy bag of chips" is a day full of as many positive comments as a bag has Cheetos. Pat your children on the back. Tell them they did something excellent. Tell them you are proud of them. Tell them they are smart and special and precious creations of God.

Just as a parent carefully slices an apple and peels the skin, cuts the core, and zips the apple up in a bag, so too do parents need to carefully "zip-lock" some careful rules within the core of their children. Peel back the normalcy and the go-with-the-flow type of child rearing the world seems to have and expose your own, God's own way, of raising children and setting rules. A child needs lines set and morals instilled. Loving discipline reminds the child of your love for him. A child without discipline is a child that does not feel loved. So as the apples are zipped up in the bag with the color-changing seal, so too do children need to be raised with life-changing morals and rules.

Change the same ol' peanut butter and jelly sandwich every now and then. Get rid of the ho-hum of lunch with a meat sandwich with lettuce or a tomato on it. In my opinion, God wants us to teach our children prayer with pizazz. Teach them to rejoice in his exciting love. Don't let them get bored with monotonous same ol' same ol' prayers. Sometimes we whisper our prayers. Sometimes we sing our prayers. Sometimes we dance and jump on the bed and clap our hands and say, "Thank You, Jesus, for everything," and that serves as our prayer. We talk about how God hears us no matter how we pray. He hears us when we sing. He hears us when we whisper. He hears us when we laugh and when we cry. God always hears our prayers and he always listens no matter how we pray. A peanut butter and jelly sandwich sets the foundation and is fine every now and then, but don't let your children get bored with the same ol' type of sandwich, I mean prayer, every time.

A Capri Sun is great to wash down lunch so go ahead and pack one for your kids. I plan on doing the same when my children are older. It is just as important to pack our children's hearts with the blood of Jesus in order to wash away their sin. It is only Jesus' blood that helped me to overcome my childhood. It is only through the blood of Jesus that I have come to understand that some people just never had anyone show them God's instructions for packing a bag.

Jesus wants every child to leave their house with a fully packed heart. He wants every child to feel like their parent took enough time to make sure they had all their goodies. Understanding the power of prayer, understanding God's love for them, understanding that Jesus quenches the parched soul, understanding that he can help them grow to be excellent parents, all these things are within the hearts of children packed by parents who read God's instructions. So pack your children's lunches with care, but more importantly, pack their hearts with the loving knowledge of God.

PACKED HEARTS ∾

"Velveeta cheese!"

"Yes, I'm so excited!"

"Do you have an awesome sandwich?

or did you just get slighted?"

"Was your mom or dad too tired

to pack you a fancy lunch?"

"Well, hey, don't worry, here,

have my Capri Sun fruit punch."

"I wish for your sake

you had mozzarella string cheese.

Don't cry, here's my napkin,

take it to wipe your tears please."

"Oh yeah, it says 'I love you' on it,

my mom can be a nerd."

"You don't have my kind of packed lunch,

but your prayers

are still heard."

"My mom says funny things like,

God packs our hearts every day

so that when we are older

we won't lose our way.

Does your mom say stuff like that?"

"Hey, here, do you want my apple?

My mom peeled the skin off

'cause she said she's setting an example."

B UT GROW IN THE GRACE AND KNOWLEDGE
of our Lord and Savior Jesus Christ. To him be
glory both now and forever! Amen.

II PETER 3:18

CHAPTER SEVENTEEN

IN THE MIDDLE

At the risk of poorly imitating a stand-up comedian, I'll say that "A funny thing happened to me on the way to finishing this book." As you know from the introduction I am a busy full-time student and mother. Things have been hard and hectic, but I was aware of the light at the end of my tunnel. I was in my Senior year as an English major and I was counting down the days until graduation. Well, sometimes God decides that there are other things one needs to be doing.

Birth control in America is quite efficient, but not always. As my doctor informed me, "Only abstinence is 100 percent effective, everything else is only 99.9 percent effective." So, he smiled and added that I was the .1 percent of the population in America that modern science did not choose to cooperate with. I am not a woman of science, nor do I believe that things happen unless God has a purpose. So, with my second child due sometime around June, I am now going to school part-time, drinking decaf coffee, and I'm sleeping much more. Wow!

I pouted like a spoiled brat and cried on and off for three weeks. (My husband however, informed me that I was still in the crying phase of the news around the five-month mark.) Heck, isn't pregnancy in general a crying phase? Facing a serious change in plans and routine was enough to throw me for a loop. I couldn't imagine that God wanted me to slow down and not graduate in the next year. I couldn't believe God was giving me another child! After my swollen frog eyes faded down and after I quit crying every time I thought about it, I reminded myself that God has a plan. And so I daydreamed as any other writer would that God wanted me to slow down, enjoy life more, and finish my book.

My grandmother informed me that "there's nothing you can do about birth and death, so you may as well enjoy it in the middle." I believe with great conviction that God is changing my life so that I may change others.

IN THE MIDDLE ~

In the middle of a cake

the pudding is so very moist.

In the middle of a day

to take a nap would be the choice.

In the middle of a walk

it's good to sit upon a rock

and contemplate your life

and lose yourself in thought.

In the middle of the night

it's good to look upon the stars

to drink some hot coffee

and consider where in life you are.

In the middle of making a decision

it's fun to roll the dice,

to flip a coin and laugh

but more importantly—to talk to Christ.

In the middle of one's life

as we run here and there

as we work for all the "things" we "need"

do we stop to think in prayer?

In the middle of hard times

it's not good to throw one's self down

and pout and remain stubborn

forgetting about the one who wears the crown.

In the middle of one's charted journey

plans are made and bags are packed

What if in the middle—

you realize you have the wrong map?

What if God chose to re-route your vacation

passing by the beach in Florida

and what if God told you that you

were destined for OKLAHOMA?!

You must go, you must not whine

for whining is not allowed

and only real babies in this life

gather admiration crowds.

If you want to be a leader

and show God's gracious light

You must be willing IN THE MIDDLE

to try to understand your plight.

For in the middle of a cake

in the middle of a day

in the middle of troubles God is there

to say:

"Eat the cake, I tried it, it's delish.

Take a nap if you're tired, but only if

you're done with your list."

And in the middle of your troubles in the middle

of your goals

God may redirect you

for the good of your soul.

THEREFORE, SINCE WE ARE SURROUNDED BY such a great cloud of witnesses, let us throw off everything that hinders and the sin that so easily entangles, and let us run with persever-ance the race marked out for us. Let us fix our eyes on Jesus, the author and perfecter of our faith, who for the joy set before him endured the cross, scorning its shame, and sat down at the right hand of the throne of God.

HEBREWS 12:1-2

CHAPTER EIGHTEEN

THANK YOU

I remember daydreaming about my adult life when I was a child. I remember daydreaming about my future husband and how wonderful he was going to be. "Tall, dark, and handsome, and he'll just love me to pieces." We all did it. We'd play those silly "folded paper open, close, open, shut, pick a number, pick a type of house, a type of car" games. Secretly, my wishes went a little further than that. My husband won't drink and be mean, my husband won't hit, my husband will be so wonderful to our children, my husband. I remember being so miserably sad as a child because my father was long since gone and because my mom was as sad and as scared as I. As a child I had heard that if you pray and ask, you will receive. That was pretty simple so I prayed. I remember being confused and very angry to find out that I had asked that God would take my awful stepfather away and I asked that I'd be happy, but I still woke up in the same bed with the same awful situation. I was so mad that I had asked and that I had not received. I didn't understand all this "God stuff."

I was twenty-five and working tediously on an Excel spreadsheet for the senior partner. I had to recreate a spreadsheet listing all the firm's expenses. It was just me, a stack of checkbook stubs a mile high, and a senior partner waiting to see if we had recouped all of our expenses through billing the

clients. I told myself to calm down and to just handle one entry
at a time, but the stack was still huge. The pile of checkbook
stubs only seemed to grow instead of get smaller. Sometimes
one entry would send me on a wild-goose chase through the
files to make sure that so-and-so hadn't double-paid, we hadn't
double-billed, or that I put it on the right "Johnson" file.
Tediously, I worked and worked and worked. About halfway
through the pile something hit me! This pile of check book
stubs had come to represent much more than just "firm costs"!
Suddenly, I realized that this pile of checkbook stubs was a
tangible example of the long years of my childhood. As a child
I had prayed and prayed and prayed, but my pain and my life
never changed and it seemed that Jesus never even seemed to
"put a dent in" my awful situation. I knew I had been blessed
in my adult life and I was thankful, but I had never really
reflected upon each prayer that I had as a child and each tear
that I had cried as a child. Somewhere in the middle of the huge
stack of checkbook stubs I was reminded that God had heard
and that God had wiped my eyes. Just as I was slowly and
tediously working on those million or so checkbook stubs, so
too was God slowly, but surely, working at fixing my awful
situation. Year by year and prayer by prayer God was bringing
me to a much better place. He wasn't going to wave his right
index finger and "beam me up" to a better childhood, but he
was going to bless me with a wonderful marriage and two
beautiful children, a mortgage on a house with a Jesus painting
that my husband bought me hanging in the entry, and a sign in
the garden that reads, "God bless this house." God did answer
my prayers! God doesn't always work as quick as lightning and
we get frustrated, we even get mad. I was mad as a silly child
who didn't understand God's ways.

My husband is all that I wished for as a child. He's the most
wonderful father any child could wish for. He's thoughtful, he
instills confidence in our daughter. He believes in hard work.
He doesn't drink or do any of those awful other things I
witnessed as a child. He's the perfect height, he's dark, and he's
so very handsome. The best part is that he does "love me to

pieces." God has blessed me so much with him that I thank God every day that my children have such a wonderful father and that I have such a loving and supportive husband. I've gotten tears of joy in my eyes too many times to count when I thank God for Brian. I realize just how awesome God is when I realize how far God has brought me and how much God has blessed me. The love I have in my adult life far outweighs the pain I had as a child and I'm so very thankful!

THANK YOU ∾

Words cannot express my thanks to you, my Jesus.

My tears of joy can try

To let you know my gratitude

My prayers of praise and singing

Say thanks that you've already worn these shoes.

Sometimes just silence

Is all I have to offer

Thanking you that you've always heard my prayers

And that you've never faltered.

Pure amazement at your power

Is all I have sometimes

And I sit with all the others

And break the bread and drink the wine.

Speechless, speechless, speechless,

Your presence is so great

Thank you that you hear all prayers

And answer every time, though we sometimes think

you answer late.

I know you always hear us

You've proven how well you listen

Thank you that you hear silence

So no need of ours is missing.

A long way you've brought me

A long way I plan to go

For Jesus, you are faithful

I pray, I love, I know.

❧

I SOUGHT THE LORD, AND HE ANSWERED me; he delivered me from all my fears. Those who look to him are radiant; their faces are never covered with shame. This poor man called, and the Lord heard him; he saved him from out of his troubles. The angel of the Lord encamps around those who fear him, and he delivers them. Taste and see the Lord is good; blessed is the man who takes refuge in him.

PSALM 34:1-8

CHAPTER NINETEEN

"Good Morning, This Is God"

Let me please expand, if I may, on my introduction to this book. I worked full-time, I slept less than half the time, and at one time I actually fell asleep studying and knocked my coffee all over my homework. Since algebra and trigonometry were the subjects that I was studying one particular night, I set my study area up in the living room. The dining room table was not large enough for five miles of notes, my book, my solutions manual, my homework, and a huge cup of coffee. I was, therefore, set up on the living room floor. Somehow during the study session, my book became my pillow and my miles of notes became my blanket, or I became their blanket. I woke up at 3:01 A.M. with my foot in a puddle of coffee (some of the coffee had absorbed into the carpet, the rest of the coffee had puddled nicely on my homework, which happened to be due that day). It was many nights like these and it was many homework assignments and research papers that kept me up until the wee hours of the morning.

One night I was typing away at the computer working madly to finish a paper that was due that day. It was quiet enough to hear my eyelids drop shut. I was forcing them to remain open as

I had a degree to earn and this paper was going to bring me one step closer to that degree. Yep, it was just me, my keyboard: "clickity click click, rap tee taa tapp tapp." My fingers sounded like a fingertip version of "River Dance," and boy was I ever making that keyboard smoke. I heard someone, though. I heard someone say "Jacob." I stopped finger-tap dancing on the keyboard and I looked around. Nobody was there. I heard it again. This time there was no doubt in my mind that God had spoken and that God had said, "Jacob." I immediately started reasoning with God. "Oh no, I'm not pregnant, I'm not having a son, I don't even like the name Jacob, besides, I'm graduating soon, I already have a child, it's already hard trying to work and go to school, I'm not pregnant. I haven't missed a pill!" I kept on typing. I ignored all the signs. I was comforted when my doctor told me that I was not pregnant, my body was just under a lot of stress. Every now and then I thought about hearing the name Jacob and I talked myself into ignoring it. Ignoring things does not make them go away. Six weeks or so later, I skipped my 10:00 A.M. class and walked over to Grady Hospital which is two blocks from Georgia State University. Guess what they told me? The nurse said, "Because you told me there must be something strange going on with your body and that you were 99 percent sure you were not pregnant, I checked the sample and the results twice, but you are pregnant!"

A couple of months later I realized that I had wanted my degree so much that I forgot to ask God what he wanted for my life. God told me what he wanted, but I was not listening. It took God giving me my surprise blessing, my son Jacob, to wake me up to his will in my life.

If you happen to be sitting up in the middle of the night and the whole rest of the house is asleep, try something for me and for your sake. Say the name "Jacob" very quickly and a little loud. It has an uncanny way of sounding like "Wake up." I learned a much more important lesson than any college textbook could offer me. I learned that if God wants your attention he'll get it one way or another. If you don't listen, don't worry, he'll make sure he is heard, he'll do what most fathers would do, he'll get your attention even if he has to force you to listen.

I realized a very hard lesson when I got pregnant with Jacob. God taught me something that I will never forget. I cannot plan my life right down to the exact minute detail. I cannot just trot along with my own plans and expect God to grant all my wishes. I have to stop and ask God what his will is in my life. I have to stop and listen. I was shocked, devastated, and surprised that God wanted me to *not* graduate this summer, that God wanted me to carry a child and give birth *again*, and that God had already named my son Jacob. I was amazed that I did not always get to be in control. I realized in the deepest sense possible that God is in control of my life and that he is in turn in control of every day of my life. It was a hard, yet important, lesson to learn.

My best friend's mother sent me a wonderful "notice" in the mail. It read: "Good morning, this is God, I'll be handling your day today, I don't need your help. Have a nice day." I put it on my fridge as a reminder to myself that I'm not the only one living my life and that I'm not the one in charge of my day, God is.

"GOOD MORNING, THIS IS GOD." ~

"I'll be in charge of your day today,

don't fret and worry,

just let me handle things my Way.

The interview? The bill, the sickness?

The car problem?

Geez, I told you once, I'll tell you again.

Your day is mine,

I'll solve 'em.

It does you no good to fret,

to stress out, to cry

but if you must I'll hold your hand,

I'll pat your back, although I wish you'd quit

asking 'why?'

There's a reason, it's a test, it's allowed sometimes

that you endure some pain,

but please child, listen . . .

Heaven is yours to gain.

I've gone before you, I've worn your shoes

I've cried the tears, I've felt the pain,

I did all this so that your life

Would not be lived in vain.

Good morning, this is God, the same one who parted

the Red Sea,

the same one who Zacchaeus climbed the

tree to see,

the same God who endured all temptation

but never sinned.

Good morning, good morning,

Let your day begin."

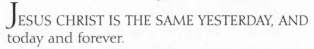

JESUS CHRIST IS THE SAME YESTERDAY, AND
today and forever.

HEBREWS 13:8

CHAPTER TWENTY

WITHOUT

My grandma is a beautiful lady. I've never imagined my grandma as being any older than forty-five. However, since my own mother is in her forties now and I'm twenty-five, Grandma would have to have aged as well. She really hasn't aged, though. Her hair is still jet black (a little help from Clairol never hurt anyone), her eyes are ice blue, and she has a wonderful smile. When my grandma was younger people used to mistake her for Elizabeth Taylor. Grandpaw used to tell a story about how he and Grandma got into a party or a restaurant simply because they thought they were being graced by Elizabeth Taylor's presence. Grandma raised two stepchildren, three grandchildren, three of her own children, and then she turned around and helped raise me and my two brothers. She is currently raising her two great-grandsons whom she and Grandpaw adopted when the boys were babies. It's a long, complicated story, but needless to say, Grandma has never been one to turn anyone away.

She says quite often that if she had to do it all over again she'd go to law school. She even says if she was "a little bit younger" she'd go now. Grandma was raised in Sweetwater, Texas. Her father worked on the railroad and he did quite well for his family. At the age of eighteen, Grandma decided that she needed to strike out on her own. She went to Seattle,

Washington, to work for Boeing. She told me once that she used to write letters home, all of which were in rhyme. Her father loved her poetry but he wondered when she was going to write a nonrhyming letter. I guess maybe I inherited some of Grandma's poetic verse. Grandma has told me one thing over and over again all my life. She always says, "Well, you can do it, ya know, you can do it." It's a pretty simple concept, really. It also works. If you tell yourself you can do something, well, then, you just do it. "I can't" has never been part of Grandma's vocabulary. I'm thankful that she taught me such a simple but powerful concept.

From boot camp to college to motherhood to today, I've realized that the same concept that Grandma has been saying for years is relevant no matter where in life you are. I'm going to take my grandmother's advice and I'm going to continue to tell myself "I can." I call my grandma all the time just to hear her tell me "I can." The world is a little large, a little scary, and it's full of battles every day. Every day the world says, "You can't." I'm thankful that my grandma had the courage to leave Sweetwater, Texas, at the age of eighteen and I'm thankful that she taught me that "I can" conquer my circumstances, "I can do it, I just can." I've added a lot to Grandma's saying, though: "I can do it, I just can. As long as I have God in my life, I can do it, I just can!" (I love you, Grandma!)

WITHOUT ∿

I've gone without certain

Things and people.

But I turned that word around.

Out with the truth is what

I mustered

And no longer was

I flustered.

I wasn't without because

You were with me

I wasn't without because I had

So many other blessings.

My past has brought me

One assurance,

It's given me strength and

Endurance.

"Without" HA!

For one can't miss what

One never had

God is wise, he knows what to give

And when and how to give it

So, if you are without for now

Be careful how you perceive it.

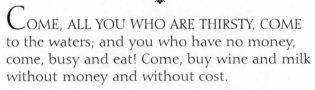

COME, ALL YOU WHO ARE THIRSTY, COME
to the waters; and you who have no money,
come, busy and eat! Come, buy wine and milk
without money and without cost.

ISAIAH 55:1

CHAPTER TWENTY-ONE

JOB

As if my surprise pregnancy was not enough to put the average person in a snug white jacket with cute buckles all the way around it, and as if my surprise pregnancy was not enough to land someone in a room with quaintly decorated white padded walls, I got a pregnancy rash! What is a pregnancy rash, you ask? I'll tell you. I did not make it up. During a pregnancy we all know that a woman's hormones are slightly off kilter. Toward the end of a pregnancy the hormones become even crazier and a woman can develop an allergic reaction to the hormonal war going on in her body. It's not surprising that I would be one of those women whose body just freaked out at the end. It's not surprising that my hormones eventually "lost it" since my mind had already been battling with my pregnancy enough to change my name to Mrs. Schwartzkoff.

The rash started out as a little spot on my knee. It grew up and down my leg for two days and then suddenly on the third day it seemed to be everywhere. It itched. It itched like a million ants on an anthill. I called my obstetrician's office. They told me that since it was a skin problem I'd need to see my regular doctor and my regular doctor would probably send me to a dermatologist. At this point my obstetrician had no idea that I had a pregnancy rash because pregnancy rashes are pretty rare. My obstetrician just imagined I was "probably camping and hiking on Mt. Everest, cliff climbing, mountain dirt biking, and such." You know, the kind of activity that all eight-month-pregnant ladies do? And during all my activity I probably just got a hold of some POISON IVY! I exaggerate this crazy joke because my obstetrician ignored me in the worst sense of the word and I was not impressed. I went to my regular doctor so that she could look at me and not know what it was and so that she could bill the insurance company $130 and bill me my $10 only to give me the name and phone number of a dermatologist and send me on my merry itching way.

Of course, every dermatologist on my plan was booked up at least until two months after my due date! My wonderful mother-in-law gave me $150 and told me to go see any dermatologist who would see me. I went to a dermatologist in downtown Atlanta who, of course, was not on my medical plan. He gave me prescriptions for a steroid and some serious anti-itch cream. I had already spent $175 on creams from Eckerd and nothing was working. My dermatologist tried to call my obstetrician and verify that these steroids would be okay for the baby, but surprise, nobody answered the phone even though they were supposedly open. It was, after all, 8:30 and the office was supposed to open at 8:30! My dermatologist told me to call my obstetrician and get permission before I got the steroid prescription filled, and he wished me luck. Well, since every hour, every half hour, every 15 minutes, every 10 minutes, every 9, 8, 7, 6, 5, 4, 3, 2 minutes, every 60, 59, 58, 57, 56, 55, 54, 53, 52, 51, 50, 49, 48, 47, 46, 45, 44, 43, 42, 41, 40, 39, 38, 37, 36, 35, 34, 33, 32, 31, 30, 29, 28, 27, 26, 25, 24, 23, 22, 21, 20, 19, 18, 17, 16, 15, 14, 13, 12, 11, 10 – 9 – 8- 7- 6- 5-4-3-2, every second of my life I was itching and wanting to cry . . . and since I had scabs that bled at will in the really inflamed areas of my rash, and since I was beyond the point of livid, I drove straight to my obstetrician's office. I had dried-up Eckerd anti-itch cream on my skin that was peeling off in places, I had red dots, and bleeding scabs on every part of me, except my face, and I walked straight into the waiting room. The room was full of pregnant women at various stages, older women who were there for various reasons, younger women who weren't pregnant, and it was now graced with my presence. I walked up to the window and the cute bubbly nurse said, "Please

sign in," "I'm not signing in and I'm not waiting, I want a doctor
and I want a doctor *now*!" "Mrs. Seymour, what seems to be the
problem?" I've heard of stupid questions, but this one really took
the cake and won the blue ribbon at the county fair!

"What seems to be the problem?" I reiterated. "I'll tell you
the problem!" I have been ignored, told to take over-the-counter
Benadryl, I've gotten lame excuses and answering machines as
a remedy for this rash, I can't sit, I can't sleep, I paid big money
to see a dermatologist not on my plan because y'all blew me off
for days before you told me to go see my regular doctor, and
now I have a prescription for steroids that some nice doctor in
downtown Atlanta gave me, but a doctor here needs to verify
that I can take it, and since y'all don't want to answer your
phone at 8:30 when you are supposed to be open, I drove here
. . . What's wrong? I'll tell you what's wrong, I want a doctor,
and I want a doctor now, and unless he's ready to schedule me
for an emergency C-section, which I highly recommend, I
suggest that you get me a doctor and I suggest that he verify
whether or not I can take this steroid so that I can sleep and I
suggest that this all happen before I legally change my name to
Job!" Two nurses practically pulled me through the window as
I was expressing my frustration very loudly. The same cute
bubbly nurse that kept telling me to take over-the-counter
Benadryl every time I called greeted me with a smile and held
my arm and escorted me through the door. I thought that if I
threw a big enough fit they would schedule me for a C-section
and this whole pregnancy along with the rash would be over.
They wouldn't schedule me for a C-section.

To make a long story short, oops, too late, I'll tell you that my
obstetrician approved the steroid and I took it. Three days later I
was able to sleep again. I still have scars from some of the scabs
and I'll never forget the torture I experienced during that rash.
During my hideous rash experience I was laying with a tank top,
my underwear, and my huge belly with anti-itch cream on every
inch of me, on my couch, and I was praying to God. "God, Jacob
must be something pretty special, because this 'pre-birth parade,
i.e., rash' has been something else!" I can't imagine how Job felt.
I only have a rash and that poor man had boils "from the sole of

his foot to the crown of his head" (Job 2:7), lost his home and his entire family! Even though none of these horrible things had happened to me I still cried out for mercy. I still felt like Job. "Why me, dear God, why me???!!!" "Please make it go away." "I can't even cry anymore, I can't even think anymore, all I can do is pray for your mercy, please, dear God, take it away, I'll behave, I'll quit pouting about this pregnancy . . . please." Since I was reminded of Job, I remembered that Job praised God's name throughout his whole ordeal. I remembered that even Job's wife told him to curse God and Job refused to curse God. Job's wife spoke to him without faith in chapter 2 of Job. "Do you still hold fast to your integrity? Bid God farewell and die." But he replied to her, "You talk as one of the foolish women would talk. Are we to receive only what is good from God, and are we to receive no misfortune?" In all this Job did not sin with his lips.

Wow! Job was a bigger man than I was at this moment. I did come to understand one thing while I was waiting for the steroids to fix my rash and while I was waiting for my due date to get closer. I realized that there was a bigger picture that had already been painted by the master painter. I realized that whatever picture I thought I had drawn and created was really only a rough draft that needed much refining. God takes care of refining our rough drafts; we have to let him. I knew somehow that God was teaching me that my soon-to-be-born son would be a huge bountiful blessing and that somehow this pregnancy rash would help me appreciate my new son, God, and my life that much more.

JOB 〜

Job was a man

Who suffered great

Satan wanted to ruin him

And seal his fate

But Job stood strong in God

He was tested

And he won

And thus a story of faith

Had begun.

You can't please God without faith

So you must sometimes search deep

Within your soul

For a belief which is concrete.

If you are standing on the Rock

You know regardless of the sea

That God will save you

For great is his mercy.

When you find yourself

Distraught, in pain, without a hope

Read the book of Job,

Look to God, and cope.

❖

AND SO HE DIED, OLD AND FULL OF YEARS.

JOB 42:17

CHAPTER TWENTY-TWO

ALL THINGS

After I had my first child I was amazed at the responsibility that women have in society. Even though my husband was a huge and wonderful help, I realized that I was the "mom" and, therefore, I had to do the majority of the work. It made sense all of a sudden why we, the women, carry a child in our womb for nine months! We still do nine times the work when the baby arrives. This sounds terrible coming from me because I have the world's most wonderful husband. Brian even gave Faith her first bath. He "does" doctor appointments (by himself sometimes), he "does" dinner, outside time, and give-Mom-a-break time. It doesn't matter that women burned bras in the sixties, though, because the "support" of the household still weighs heavy on our shoulders. After I gave birth to my first child I was shocked about the 75 percent of household responsibility that I had to now carry out.

Three years later, tangled up with a lot of "lessons"and a lot of prayers I realize now that the role of the mother is not only a huge role, but more so, it is a huge honor. A mother can make or break her household. If Mom walks in the door in control, calm, cool, and collected, and with God on her mind, her household will respond in the same way. If Mom walks in the door, forgetting to count to ten, forgetting to pray, and forgetting God, forgetting the cool and calm part, well, then, you can just forget it because her family will respond in the same way. When this happens the evening and everyone's nerves are shot. I realized all this about three months after Jacob was born. I had adjusted to the two-child household, recovery of birth, and going back to work. I realized I had to adjust to the "coming home from work" thing also. Work, traffic, and exhaustion seemed to follow me in the front door. Well, actually, we don't use our front door. Does anyone use their front door? We push the garage door opener, park, and walk into the kitchen. It seems that the only time our front door gets used is when the Girl Scouts are selling cookies and we answer their knock at the front door. Anyway, my day followed me in the kitchen door . . . (Three weeks have come and gone since I began this particular story. I was interrupted three times by Brian, Faith, and Jacob beckoning to my mother's to-do list. I usually only work on this book when it's like Christmas Eve around here and "not a creature is stirring, not even a mouse," but sometimes I get a little rebellious and try to type when the troops are awake. I attempt to write when all are awake because I was going to be a comedian at one time, and because sometimes I get a wild hair to try something crazy.)

Needless to say, 100 million events took place when I walked in the door. Faith stubbed her toe and was screaming like it had been cut off, Jacob was distraught over the fact that his pacifier had grown legs and walked away, and Brian was trying to cook a macaroni and cheese meal and fold laundry in the middle of it all. "Mommy is home, my sweet little angels," I said as the birds I had rented from *Snow White* graciously chirped on the kitchen windowsill. Funny, nobody heard me. Oh, it was utter chaos around here, no wonder!

I have witnessed a chain reaction of stress and confusion in my household when I react inappropriately to my family. I came home one day and acted exactly how I wanted to act. I acted tired and selfish. I kicked off my shoes because my feet were killing me. I ran to the bathroom because I almost got a bladder infection sitting in traffic for ninety minutes, I acted irritated when I couldn't eat at least yogurt before someone wanted something of me, I responded sharply when my husband wanted to know where some essential kid item was, and I threw a fit when I couldn't sit down and take a five-minute break before I began my role of mother and superwoman. I could have changed my name to Nellie Olsen from *Little House on the Prairie* because at that point I had mastered her brattish behavior. I watched my husband change into a stressed-out, confused, also tired and irritated individual because he was having to deal with one as well (me). I witnessed the kids react to the confusion. Fussing and whining escalated to a Mt. Everest peak and fifteen minutes into my arrival home the house was a steaming kettle ready to blow.

I've learned that I need to respond to my family the way I want them to respond to me. So, the world is on my shoulders when it comes to my family. It's up to me to remain calm and to have patience, understanding, energy, and a calm disposition when I deal with them and all their reactions to life. Well, I've come to the conclusion that I cannot act like Jesus without Jesus in my life. So if I want to respond to my family as Jesus would, I better call in the king of all kings: Jesus himself. I ask Jesus to help me be a good mother and a good wife. And he does. "I can do all things through Christ who strengthens me."

ALL THINGS ∼

All Things

Is everything you do in a day

From waking up to laundry

To little things that you say.

All things

Is exhaustion, defeat, and victory

All things is what I want

Jesus to oversee.

All things

Is all of it from the house

To the kids

All things is forgiveness

For things I wish I never did.

All things

Is all of it

Lord, it's all too much

In all things—Is where, dear Lord,

I need your touch

❖

I CAN DO EVERYTHING THROUGH HIM WHO
GIVES ME STRENGTH.

PHILIPPIANS 4:13

CHAPTER TWENTY-THREE

GOD'S REMEDY

The Lord blessed me one hundred times over when he gave me my husband Brian. Brian is a wonderful man. He's always supportive of whatever my Lucille Ball self is doing at the time. Whether I'm working on my "will be published one day" book, training to run the Peachtree Road Race, working on a paper for college, working on a sketch of the kids that resembles more an abstract picture than a realistic one, whether I'm ripping the wallpaper off the bathroom wall because I just can't wait to re-mud the walls, or whether I'm just talking too much, he patiently listens. He's an overall wonderful man. I tell him that I'm so glad he's not a caveman. A caveman, of course, is a man who still expects dinner cooking and ready by six, potpourri on the stove, the toilet paper folded in a cute triangle, and the pantry to always be stocked with Little Debbies. So, yes, the Lord blessed me one hundred times over because Brian is so wonderful.

The Lord also blessed me one hundred times over because when I married Brian, I received with him his whole family. Brian's grandmother Tina is an amazing woman. She raised four children by herself while she worked nights as a nurse. She did an amazing job. She's the woman that they coined the phrase "Been there, done that" after. I call Grandmom crying from time to time. I call Grandmom just to talk because I know she'll make me laugh. I call her because she is so amazing and because she is so full of God's love. She always helps me deal with whatever is at hand and I appreciate her so much. I'm thankful that God not only blessed me with a wonderful husband, he also iced the cake by giving me Brian's grandmom too.

When I'm seventy years old, I want to be the kind of grandmom that Tina is. I'll know I've succeeded at becoming a candle showing God's light to those around me if I become half the grandmom that Tina is.

GOD'S REMEDY ∼

God gave us grandmoms to love

he sent them here in secret

to give advice

from above.

As we struggle to understand

sometimes God whispers through her

wonderful voice,

"Don't worry about it,

for God has made this choice."

My grandmom says the wisest things

and she'll tell me when I'm wrong

she'll tell me if I'm singing

my own self-pity song.

She talks about her life, the hard times

(much harder than my own)

and I realize that this "storm" of mine

is really a spring breeze gracefully blown
my way.
Somehow being with Grandmom
is like being closer to Jesus
and so grandmoms must be here
to teach as well as heal us.
Last Sunday I think I saw my grandmom's wings
for only at Grandmom's did an inner struggle cease
and because she talked of Jesus
I left Grandmom's ready again for the world
armed with peace.
I love you, Grandmom!

LOVE IS PATIENT, LOVE IS KIND. It does not
envy, it does not boast, it is not proud. It is not
rude, it is not self-seeking, it is not easily
angered, it keeps no record of wrongs. Love
does not delight in evil but rejoices with the
truth. It always protects, always trusts, always
hopes, always perseveres.

I CORINTHIANS 13:4-7

NOW FAITH IS BEING SURE OF WHAT WE
hope for and certain of what we do not see.

HEBREWS 11:1-2

lives of two children that Jesus loved enough to die for and that Jesus loved enough to call by name.

ONCE UPON A
SUMMER AFTERNOON ∾

I played house under a tree and used a large branch

as a broom.

Once upon a fall day

I piled up leaves and landed in them

as the branch I leaped from backward swayed.

Once upon a spring

morning bright

my brother and I made toy boats

out of Grandpaw's wood and then we flew our kites.

Once upon my lifetime

as I grew and understood

I differentiated between what I wanted

and what God said I should do.

❋

I WILL GIVE YOU THE TREASURES OF darkness, riches stored in secret places, so that you may know that I am the LORD, the God of Israel, who summons you by name.

ISAIAH 45:3

QUESTIONABLE GOALS

I was working full-time and going to school full-time when I found out I was pregnant with Jacob. I was also only two semesters away from graduating when I found out I was pregnant with Jacob. I was shocked. "Who, what, where, when, why?" I asked, as I tried to regain my balance as each one of those words buzzed, flew, and zipped by my ears like Kamikaze flies headed toward flypaper. With all these questions zipping around, I started thinking and questioning my own life and my own goals. My conclusion in solving this great mystery, my pregnancy, was that God must know more than I and that maybe my goals have been questionable.

QUESTIONABLE GOALS ∾

When you dribble a ball

down a soccer field

The goal is to get the ball past

the goalie's striped shield.

When you hit a line drive

right between second and third

the goal is to run fast

and fly

like a bird.

When you stand in a three-point zone

out on the court

the goal is to make the ball "swoosh"

and not fall short.

When your life is yours and yours alone

your goals are easily shattered.

When your life is his

suddenly they matter.

❖

I TELL YOU THAT THIS MAN, RATHER THAN
the other went home justified before God. For
everyone who exalts himself will be humbled,
and he who humbles himself will be exalted.

LUKE 18:14

YOU MUST BE AN ANGEL

I have a dear Christian friend who told me I had to pray for someone who had hurt me deeply. I began to pray for that person, even though I was so hurt I did not want to. This friend is always loving people through Jesus Christ. I've learned a lot from her in the way she lives and in the way she loves. She is the person most like Jesus I have ever met and I'm so thankful to be blessed by her presence.

I have learned a very important fact in life. If you cannot love someone by yourself, if you just can't bear the thought of loving someone who has hurt you because you are too angry or just too hurt, then you have to love them through Jesus. If you just forget about trying to do it all yourself, if you just give up the battle and let Jesus love enough for both of you, then it is as good as done. I began loving someone through Jesus and slowly but surely I began to have a heart for that person, and then one day I realized I loved that person deeply. It seems that sometimes hurt and anger can cover up your love for someone. God can take the hurt and anger away and reveal the love that he initially put in that relationship. A good friend of mine once told me that "when your heart breaks for someone, you really know you are loving them through Jesus." She was right.

My mom would give you the shirt off her back. She's a lot like Jesus. She gives and gives and she doesn't ask for anything

CHAPTER TWENTY-FOUR

TRAFFIC LIGHTS

Traffic in Atlanta is atrocious. We all buzz around as if we are the only one who needs to be somewhere. We all speed up, slow down, and ride bumpers as if we are the only ones on the road and as if we should have a "no traffic hassles pass." I was in a traffic jam one day when I realized that God must feel like he's dealing with a bunch of crazy drivers sometimes when he deals with each one of us individually. We all cruise through our lives in a hurry to get somewhere. God must want to throw five red lights in our way (I'm sure he does at times) when he's frustrated at our lack of listening skills. I'm sure he'd like to just step right in the middle of our "traffic jams," i.e., our lives, and signal us to go here and there, stop, detour if we need to, etcetera, and just clear up all the traffic we either seem to create or get caught up in while we are trying to live our lives. Geez, the Lord must just be as frustrated at us for not letting him drive (steer) our lives in the proper direction as a cop on a hot humid day who is trying to steer people away from a 5:15 wreck at Spaghetti Junction in Atlanta.

TRAFFIC LIGHTS ~

Don't you just not like

those darn traffic lights

when they are red they are red forever

you may as well be in your bed for the night.

And yellow ones,

don't they mean speed up

lay your foot on the pedal

and, oh yeah, "Watch that truck!!!!"

When they are green

we know we are smooth

especially if we speed through

two in a row—

but when they are bright red

we must slow down

and stop.

Don't you dislike stopping

in the middle of your journey

especially if you are late

and really in a hurry?

When God presents a yellow light

we say, "Oh, but if I just speed up . . . "

And when he presents a green light

We say, "God, you are so great,

thanks for this car and all my other stuff!"

But God says, "No, that first light was yellow,

that green one I allowed, but now I'm demanding

that you hear me clear and loud!

This light is red, you must stop!

I've tried to give you warnings,

don't you see all the cops?"

Y OUR WORD IS A LAMP FOR MY FEET AND A
light for my path.

PSALM 119:105

CHAPTER TWENTY-FIVE

ONCE UPON A SUMMER AFTERNOON

My older brother and I are only a year and a half apart. We endured some pretty hideous, heart-breaking things in our childhood and because of that we are very close. We leaned on each other a lot. We mended each other's broken hearts when no one else could. We played and pretended awful things weren't going on around us. We stood up for each other. We protected each other from awful stepfathers and from a number of other things. We loaned each other money in high school for prom dresses, tuxes, lunch money, gas money, and whatever else teens need. We worked hard for everything we had. We could have been twins because we were both born in the same yoke of alcoholism, terror, heartache, and pain. My heart did not just break in half and disintegrate because my brother was the force that kept my heartstrings together. The fact that I had my older brother in the midst of all the pain gave me a reason to keep going. I love my brother as if he were a part of me. I love him so much because he's always been a friend to me.

I pray that my brother will realize that Jesus loves him even more than we loved each other during all the pain we endured as children. I pray that my brother will realize that Jesus loves him even more than I do today, and that's a whole lot. "Once Upon a Summer Afternoon" is just a glimpse back into my childhood and times with my brother. It's a glimpse into the lives of two children that Jesus loved enough to die for and that Jesus loved enough to call by name.

Once upon a Summer Afternoon ∼

I played house under a tree and used a large branch

as a broom.

Once upon a fall day

I piled up leaves and landed in them

as the branch I leaped from backward swayed.

Once upon a spring

morning bright

my brother and I made toy boats

out of Grandpaw's wood and then we flew our kites.

Once upon my lifetime

as I grew and understood

I differentiated between what I wanted

and what God said I should do.

❖

I WILL GIVE YOU THE TREASURES OF darkness, riches stored in secret places, so that you may know that I am the LORD, the God of Israel, who summons you by name.

ISAIAH 45:3

QUESTIONABLE GOALS

I was working full-time and going to school full-time when I found out I was pregnant with Jacob. I was also only two semesters away from graduating when I found out I was pregnant with Jacob. I was shocked. "Who, what, where, when, why?" I asked, as I tried to regain my balance as each one of those words buzzed, flew, and zipped by my ears like Kamikaze flies headed toward flypaper. With all these questions zipping around, I started thinking and questioning my own life and my own goals. My conclusion in solving this great mystery, my pregnancy, was that God must know more than I and that maybe my goals have been questionable.

QUESTIONABLE GOALS ~

When you dribble a ball
down a soccer field
The goal is to get the ball past
the goalie's striped shield.
When you hit a line drive
right between second and third
the goal is to run fast
and fly
like a bird.
When you stand in a three-point zone
out on the court
the goal is to make the ball "swoosh"
and not fall short.
When your life is yours and yours alone
your goals are easily shattered.
When your life is his
suddenly they matter.

I TELL YOU THAT THIS MAN, RATHER THAN
the other went home justified before God. For
everyone who exalts himself will be humbled,
and he who humbles himself will be exalted.

LUKE 18:14

YOU MUST BE AN ANGEL

I have a dear Christian friend who told me I had to pray for someone who had hurt me deeply. I began to pray for that person, even though I was so hurt I did not want to. This friend is always loving people through Jesus Christ. I've learned a lot from her in the way she lives and in the way she loves. She is the person most like Jesus I have ever met and I'm so thankful to be blessed by her presence.

I have learned a very important fact in life. If you cannot love someone by yourself, if you just can't bear the thought of loving someone who has hurt you because you are too angry or just too hurt, then you have to love them through Jesus. If you just forget about trying to do it all yourself, if you just give up the battle and let Jesus love enough for both of you, then it is as good as done. I began loving someone through Jesus and slowly but surely I began to have a heart for that person, and then one day I realized I loved that person deeply. It seems that sometimes hurt and anger can cover up your love for someone. God can take the hurt and anger away and reveal the love that he initially put in that relationship. A good friend of mine once told me that "when your heart breaks for someone, you really know you are loving them through Jesus." She was right.

My mom would give you the shirt off her back. She's a lot like Jesus. She gives and gives and she doesn't ask for anything in return. She just wants you to love her, which is exactly what Jesus wants. She comes over with a basket full of crafts for her and Faith to do while I'm at work. She plays on the floor with Jacob so that he doesn't feel left out from the rest of the world. She puts chicken in the Crock-Pot for dinner, she reorganizes my canned goods, Tupperware, and hall closet. She understands the struggles of raising children in a big world and her heart just keeps on giving.

It's obvious to me that angels are all around us. Some are in the form of mothers, some are in the form of friends. The more I try to love people through Jesus, the more likely it is that I will see some more of God's angels working in my life.

YOU MUST BE AN ANGEL ∾

Where are your wings?

I saw 'em, I know they are there

I saw 'em in a flash,

They sparkled with your hair.

Where is your halo?

Is it in your pocket?

Take it out.

I just know you are an angel

Beyond a shadow of a doubt.

Where is your gown?

The one with the gold lining?

The one that is beautiful,

Full of God, that's shining.

You can't hide that you're an angel.

You can't hide your disguise,

I see Jesus in you every day,

He looks at me through your eyes.

---❖---

THE LORD IS NEAR TO ALL WHO CALL ON
him, to all who call on him in truth.

PSALM 145:18

CHAPTER TWENTY-EIGHT

ONE DAY

I wrote a letter to my best friend real late one night. I was exhausted and I was enduring a lot of pressure. My letter relays all of these emotions into one tangled mess. I am adding this letter to my book unedited because letters to friends are not edited. They are real and they say what they say. This particular letter inspired me to write a poem. Therefore, the letter and the poem are presented in their original, raw, emotional form.

Dear Brenda,

Hi. How the heck are you? I'm sorry it's been so long since you've heard from me. Life is crazy. I'm so exhausted. By the time I get both kids bathed and in bed, it's practically the crack of dawn and it's time to do it all over again. Never mind the whole huge "working, grocery shopping, cooking dinner, helping Brian with his HUGE projects and student teaching stuff." Geez, Brenda, I feel like crying. So much for a funny letter, huh? If I wait until I feel rested and funny, you'll never get a letter. How's Bradley? His growth and weight are good? How's your mom? How's your recovery? I was so happy to hear that you feel great! Wow. I haven't even said that and Jacob is four months old. Actually, now that I've thought about it long enough, I do feel great. I do. I can't even believe I had a baby four months ago. It's been a long road and a lot of work, but I'm back to normal. I walk three miles and run three miles just about every day. Sometimes I skip Mondays. My workout is my only sanity, that and God, of course. I don't know how people even live their lives without God. I wouldn't even be a good person let alone be able to attempt to be a superb mom and wife. It takes a lot out of a person, this whole mom, wife thing. Doesn't it? Geez, without God, I'd be hideous at it all. Even with God sometimes I feel like I'm barely hanging on. Faith was so hilarious last night. I was reading Isaiah 45, beginning at verse 2:

"I will go before you and make the crooked places straight; I will break in pieces the gates of bronze and cut the bars of iron. I will give you the treasures of darkness and hidden riches of secret places that you may know that I, the Lord, who call you by your name, am the God of Israel. For Jacob my servant's sake, and Israel my elect, I have even called you by your name; I have named you though you have not known me. I am the Lord and there is no other."

Faith was so funny, she listened quietly, and interrupted when I said Jacob. She said, "Hey, that's Jacob's name!" Isaiah 45:8: "Rain down, you heavens from above, and let the skies pour righteousness; let the earth open, let them bring forth salvation, and let righteousness spring up together. I, the Lord, have created it." Faith said, . . . "HEY!, You are not the Lord Mom! You did not create everything! You're not God, God is!" I tried not to laugh. She was so serious. She thought I was sitting there saying everything God was saying, as if I was the Lord. It was a classic moment.

So, what's new on your end? How's Michell? How did her move go? How's your mom? I need to write her a quick note and send her a picture too. She sent me the greatest thing. A good morning statement from God. "Good morning, this is God, I'll be handling your day today. I don't need your help, so have a nice day." It goes something like that. It's on my fridge and I just love it. Your mom is so wonderful. I pray that when I'm in my forties I can be a burning candle for someone the way your mom is for me. She's such a wonderful reminder of God's faithfulness. I've been so burdened and exhausted lately, I feel like I need to call her and have her tell me to get a grip. I'm not calling anyone though, hardly anyway, because my long distance has been way too big and my expenses are crazy lately. I need $2,200 worth of work on my teeth from two $600 root canals to crowns. Brian's car is wrecked. He hit a deer. The deductible is $250. Geez, I can't even tell you the stress of money lately. It's like all of a sudden, things we never have expenses on are at large. Root canals, crowns, Brian's teaching stuff . . . Oh well, I sound awful don't I? I don't even know how I'm supposed to pay for my stationery and my business I'm trying to start. I don't even want to have the other root canal and crown done because I'd rather us have a little bit of a Christmas than spend every dime we have on my stupid teeth. GEEZ, AREN'T I JUST A SOLDIER FOR THE LORD TONIGHT!! Geez, where's my faith? At times like these I want to laugh at the fact that I have a daughter named Faith and how I'm supposed to always have faith I told myself on the way home from work the other night, or really, I told God I was sorry for being so ridiculous and that I didn't have anything to worry about or to figure out because the whole stationery thing wasn't even mine anyway. It was God's. So I just need to let God fund it. And then I laughed at myself. Little ol' me trying to make it all work by myself. What a joke. I just need to be faithful in prayer and let God work it for his good. A small something is telling me to just calm down and finish my book. Maybe my book is the answer to all my financial worries about the stationery. Then Satan jumps in there and says, "What do you think you are gonna do with this book anyway, make it big and sell copies?" Then I command Satan out of my life and I pray for the strength and the wisdom to finish my book and to let God use it for his good because he's the whole reason I'm writing it anyway. Brenda, there's always such spiritual warfare going on. It's exhausting. I carry my Bible with me wherever I go now. I read my Bible in my car before I go into work every day. The other morning I was so weak and wanted to cry. I just prayed that God would show me what I need to read that morning and that

I would have the strength to go on. I actually prayed and asked God to carry me that day because I just didn't feel strong enough to walk. Guess what I was led to read??? It's exciting really.

Ephesians 6:10. "Finally, my brethren, be strong in the Lord and in the power of his might. Put on the whole armor of God, that you may be able to stand against the wiles of the devil. For we do not wrestle against flesh and blood, but against principalities, against powers, against the rulers of the darkness of this age, against spiritual hosts of wickedness in the heavenly places. Therefore, take up the whole armor of God, that you may be able to withstand in the evil day, and having done all, to stand. Stand therefore, having girded your waist with truth, having put on the breastplate of righteousness."

Wow! Wasn't that great! I felt like I needed to carry my Bible in my purse all day, though I knew full well that I would not be able to stop and read it at work, which is why I read it in my car every morning before I go into work. Well, I felt so funny carrying my Bible in my purse. I didn't even have enough room in my purse for all my junk let alone carry my Bible in there. I did it anyway though and guess what? A friend of mine at work needed to hear the exact words I had just read! Guess what I did? I just pulled out my Bible, the same one I felt so funny about putting in my purse just five minutes earlier, and I read Ephesians 6:10 to her. She quit crying and she just looked at me like she couldn't believe it. She said the night before she was praying and God reminded her of those exact verses. She said, "God must have known I would need them today." I was so excited because God had used me. I didn't solve my friend's problems, nor were my troubles solved in two seconds, but the mere fact that God is in control was reiterated to both of us; that's what was so great!

Well, gotta run for now. God Bless!

Love,

Roller

(Life is a roller coaster and I seem to scream so loud and make such a production going "down and up hills" that Brenda calls me "Roller.")

ONE DAY ～

One day I was weak.

I prayed for strength.

One day I cried

Enough tears to fill up a fish tank.

One day I tripped

In the middle of a race,

I scuffed my knee

Never mind

What happened to my face.

One day my heart broke

For someone I hardly knew

And I wondered what could I,

One single person do.

One day I laughed

When tears just would not come

One day I walked

Because I was too tired to run.

One day I thought

That life was hard

One day I bought a friend

A greeting card.

One day I dreamt

Of dreams I desired to come true.

One day I prayed

That Jesus, I was more like you.

Full of strength and righteousness

With my armor standing fast.

One day long ago at recess

I was picked last.

One day regardless

Of it all

I can say when asked,

"Yes, I answered when you called."

GOD IS OUR REFUGE AND STRENGTH, an ever-present help in trouble.

PSALM 46:2

CHAPTER TWENTY-NINE

GRACE: GOD REIGNS AND CARES ETERNALLY

Once upon an awful Sunday morning all chaos broke loose. The hallway bathroom was still ripped apart because I had started the "project" of redoing it two months earlier. Coffee was made, two children were fed and happy, but the rest of the house was an utter disaster. Piled-up laundry on the couch to be folded, toys from the living room to the den, down the hall and back again. And my bathroom stuff consisting of paint, cabinet doors, a shower curtain and rod, and bath toys seemed to be escaping from the confines of the bathroom walls.

My husband was not impressed with the disaster and he told me about it. I was not impressed with his unimpressedness and I told him about it. I became furious for many reasons. I was upset that he had only noticed what was not done, not all the 100 million other things I had already done and the other 100 million things that I was presently doing. He had slept in until 9 A.M. and dishes were done and coffee was made, so I didn't even really see why, regardless of the mess, he could possibly find time to have a bad attitude this particular morning. Heck, I hadn't slept until 9:00 A.M. since I was sixteen years old, or at least since I had given birth! You can imagine my level of unimpressedness.

I know we are all human and though I try my darnedest to be like Jesus, I became very angry, and I said a few things I should not have. Tears of anger and hurt streamed down my face as I tried to scrub paint off the hallway floor which had escaped the bathroom by way of my heel. I thought, "Lord, how do I do it all? I can't keep the house spotless, kids happy, bathroom projects finished, bills paid, etc., and deal with a husband who is ticked ridiculously about some toys on the floor, and I can't deal with myself when I can't deal with it anymore."

I hardly talked to my husband the rest of the day. I did ask him to take the door off the hinges because I was going to paint the door, but other than that all I said was that I was going to the gym at 4:00. Seven miles later, on my way home from the gym, I cried and prayed. I prayed for grace. Grace to do it all and still have grace when I was done (or not done, which seemed to always be the case because there is always something to do). I realized as I was praying for grace that I had never prayed for grace before. "Wow!" I thought to myself. "I have prayed for so many hundreds of things. I cannot believe I have never prayed for grace." I was so surprised by this small tidbit that I began to focus on what grace was and how it could be applied to my life. I decided that I would write a poem entitled "Grace." Of course, my life was hectic and I didn't quite get to writing the poem until a few days later.

A few days later I was telling a good Christian friend about my awful Sunday morning and she quietly listened. She smiled at me and just looked at me like she understood. I had not mentioned the part about praying for grace. I was having too much fun adding humor to the whole Sunday morning scene. I told her that making coffee and doing the dishes was not enough to keep my husband happy, but if the Beatles were playing in the background, if coffee, a Danish, and the Sunday paper were sitting on the dining room table, if the house was spotless, potpourri was simmering on the stove, and if I had rented the birds from the *Snow White* movie to sing on the windowsill for the morning, well, then, it would be a happy day, and then and only then could I paint my bathroom and try to finish something that I wanted to. Fortunately for myself, at some point I quit talking long enough to take a breath and let her comment. Her first comment was, "Kristina, God will give you grace to handle it all." I almost fell over! I had not even mentioned grace to her or that I had prayed for grace. I told her that it was amazing that she used the word "grace" because I was on the verge of writing a poem about grace.

Sometimes it takes a few days for a new poem to transpire. "Grace" was not written overnight nor was "Grace" inspired by one event. My good Christian friend is presently facing many heartbreaking situations in her own life. Finances, a sick husband, and exhaustion from working two jobs are just the surface issues at hand in her life. I heard her leave a voice mail message for her best friend one day and it broke my heart. Her voice was just so tired as she left a brief message about how much she missed her and wished she had more time to spend with her. Her heart was just so heavy as she left word canceling their after-Thanksgiving-Day shopping plans because she would have to work her second job. My heart broke as she spoke of her husband's troubles. "Geez!" I thought to myself. "What do I ever have to complain about? Here is this poor exhausted lady who just loves the Lord so much and she's trying so hard to make it all work!" I had to leave the office and go cry and pray for her. My heart broke for her. That message she left for her best friend was an example of living one's life with "grace." "Through it all, I thought to myself, she is living her life with grace."

I went to the bathroom with a pen and a scratch piece of paper. I got down on my knees and I prayed. I wrote the poem "Grace" just as quickly as my fingers are typing on this page. I had written "grace" on the top of the page before I started writing the poem and when I wrote the last word of the poem I looked up at the title. Do you know what God said to me at that exact moment? God reigns and cares eternally. The first letter of each word spells out "grace."

God is slowly but surely showing me how to have grace in my life no matter what the circumstance. I gave my mom a coffee cup with a picture of a lady with curlers in her hair, a bathrobe, slippers, a coffee cup in her hand, an ironing board in the background, and piles of laundry everywhere. One side of the coffee cup reads, "Heaven just keeps looking better and better, doesn't it? The other side of the coffee cup reads, "Be joyful always, pray continually, give thanks in all circumstances, for this is God's will for you in Christ Jesus." (1 Thessalonians 5:16:18)

I'm working at applying that verse as well as grace to my life.

GRACE: GOD REIGNS AND CARES ETERNALLY ∼

Lord, please help me

To have grace today

To understand your will

In things I do and what I pray.

Lord, it is not easy

For your own son questioned you

Lord, just give me grace

Today in all I do.

I need grace

For strength alone is not enough.

I need grace

Because without it handling today

Is just too tough.

I need grace along with patience

Grace along with tears

Grace along this journey

Of trials, tribulations, and fears.

Lord, the world can feel

As heavy as a mountain

Lord, please shower grace upon me

As if it were a fountain.

Lord, today

It's simple:

Jesus saved my life.

Now I just pray for grace

To handle any strife.

Grace

I pray for just a little here and there

To help me endure

Life's wear

and tear.

❖

LET US THEN APPROACH THE THRONE OF grace with confidence, so that we may receive mercy and find grace to help us in our time of need.

HEBREWS 4:16

MY GRACE IS SUFFICIENT FOR YOU, FOR my power is made perfect in weakness.

2 CORINTHIANS 12:9

CHAPTER THIRTY

SEEK YE FIRST THE KINGDOM OF GOD

I was looking for my disk with my book on it one night when I came across one of my husband's disks. The title on the label read "Key to Happiness." I thought to myself, "Isn't that interesting, maybe I should put this disk in instead." It would be simple if life was that easy. Then I realized that people go through their lives looking for the key to happiness in all the wrong places. People call up the psychics as if they will find all the answers to their life. People watch hideous talk shows looking for entertainment; who knows what they are looking for on those talk shows. They only find lewd entertainment, and how can that make them happy? People look for happiness in shopping malls, in extra hours at work, in alcohol, or in food. People everywhere are looking for happiness instead of looking for God. The great thing about God is that one does not even have to search for him because he's always there waiting for his children to call out his name.

I thought of myself as well. I look for happiness in goals. If I can just set one more goal and accomplish one more thing, whether that thing is a degree that I'm desperately trying to earn or whether I'm trying to find a level of peace within my own life of chaos. "Seek ye first the kingdom of God and all these things will be added to you." That is the key, my friends, and I am trying to remind myself of that every day. The more that I let go and let God, the more sense my life seems to make.

SEEK YE FIRST
THE KINGDOM OF GOD ∼

And all these things will be added unto you.

For God wants you to listen

To what it is he wants you to do.

Don't run around looking for a magic key

To unlock a life of riches, for real wealth is

only found in eternity.

The Key to Happiness cannot be duplicated

Or found on a label

The Key to Happiness sits alone

Atop a bountiful table.

A man left it there

While he went to get the dinner dishes

The Key to Happiness belongs to a man

Who during the day and night fishes.

This man never tires

He just keeps on

Working and singing a song.

But for now he has laid the key on the table

For anyone who's curious

And able

Can try the key

And unlock their soul.

When will your last supper be?

Dinner is ready: Have some soup, here's a bowl.

❖

BUT SEEK FIRST HIS KINGDOM AND HIS righteousness, and all these things will be given to you as well. Therefore do not worry about tomorrow, for tomorrow will worry about itself. Each day has enough trouble of its own.

MATTHEW 6:33

I WILL GIVE YOU THE KEYS OF THE KINGDOM of heaven; whatever you bind on earth will be bound in heaven, and whatever you loose on earth will be loosed in heaven.

MATTHEW 16:19

I AM THE LIVING ONE; I WAS DEAD, AND behold I am alive for ever and ever! And I hold the keys of death and Hades.

REVELATION 1:18

CHAPTER THIRTY-ONE

WHAT?

I n 1995 my husband and I finished our terms in the armed forces, had our first child, started college, and moved cross-country from Washington State (my original roots) to Georgia (Brian's original roots). We decided that we wanted Faith to grow up around her grandparents and we were going to need all the help we could get since we were going to work and go to college full-time. I was twenty-one years old and although I had served four years in the air force, I was still gullible, naive, and clueless as far as knowing "how the world operated." I got a job as a receptionist at a law firm two or three days after we arrived. I remember calling my grandparents to tell them about this wonderful job that paid (don't laugh hysterically) $17,000, but since I asked for $18,000 a year, I received $18,000 a year! Wow! I thought I had really accomplished something when I was offered this job. I think that salary was way below the average level of poverty, but I did not know it at the time. I was thankful for anything.

The job was hideous in every sense of the word. One of the attorneys "buzzed" me when his $200 pen would run out of ink and asked me to bring him a refill. Another attorney "buzzed" me when he wanted a fresh cup of coffee. I accidentally put sugar in his coffee instead of Sweet'N Low and he said, "Kristina, I'd rather get cancer than get fat, so put Sweet'N Low, not sugar, in my coffee." And he handed it back to me. "Okay," I thought to myself. I ordered all the supplies, greeted all the clients, got the mail, typed, took dictation, learned Word Perfect, went to the bank sometimes because the CPA was usually out of the country or else she was at the building site of her lodge. If I had been a rug I would have been ready for the junkyard. I was frayed and worn out. They walked all over me whenever they could and I took it and said, "Yes, sir." They understood golf and sleek black luxury cars more than they understood my present position in life so I did not take it personally. They thought I was amazing and I appreciated their thoughts rather than choosing to hate their actions.

Most of the secretaries were wonderfully nice—except for one, of course. She put a package of original documents in the wrong pile one day and she blamed me for the error. She meant to place her package in the "overnight" pile, but she placed it in the regular mail pile. I had gone to lunch and I was not there when the mailman picked up the regular mail pile. Regardless, she was furious with me and told me I better go to the post office and dig through all the mail until I found it and if I couldn't find it, I might as well not come back. So I did. I went down to the post office and dug and dug. Everyone felt so bad for me. Three other post office workers looked with me, but to no avail. Of course, I was a mother and a student as well as a full-time receptionist "rug," so the pressure I felt every day was enough to make me snap. I did not snap, though, I just prayed. I told myself that this job was incentive to graduate no matter how awful it was at the time.

Fortunately, all the experience at this awful job gave me experience to try bigger and better things. I went on an interview for a legal secretarial position in a one-man office. The attorney I interviewed with was so nice. He could not believe how articulate and professional I was. He was so excited to hire me except he wanted to give me a "tape" and see how I did. I could have fainted. I had never operated one of those Dictaphone machines! I was used to taking dictation with the attorney standing behind me and walking around while I typed. I had never run one of those sewing machine foot-pedal machines. What was I going to do? I told him that I'd be glad to try, but that I had not operated one before. Geez, *Candid Camera* should have been there. *America's Funniest Home Videos* would have had the tape of the century! I was a babbling fool. I was so nervous that I could not even slow down and concentrate. My thoughts were running over each other like a stampede as I was trying desperately to focus. I heard him say, "Good, she types fast." I can imagine what he thought when he got close enough to look at what I was typing:

December 8, 1995
To: Avionics Flight
(I couldn't hear the address nor could I figure out the volume on the machine while the tape kept playing, nor could I figure out how to stop it and start it over or rewind) 1234 I don't know what the street was . . .

Dear Judge Whaopper,

I have enlosed a ocpy of the dedde ertificate as well a s a detailed description of the legal description of the cargog fliht rules Volume II,chp 3 pg 4 . . .

I think an eternity must have passed. It may have only been ten minutes. The man was so nice. He said to just relax and calm down and that he was sure I was just nervous and the machine was new to me. He wanted me to try it again. He must have given me five tries. I think he desperately wished that I was as wonderful on the machine as I was during the regular interview. I may as well have had roller skates, a clown costume, and deer antlers on my head. I was a spaz. I could not regain my composure. Once something like that happens to me the momentum of the disaster just picks up until I crash. I finally stopped trying to wrestle with the machine. Since I was wrestling with the machine so "nicely," the World Wrestling Federation walked in for a brief moment and asked me if I wanted a job with them instead. I sweetly declined the job at

WWF. I just told the attorney I was sorry for wasting his time. He tried to compliment me and he told me it was fine and that I was just a little inexperienced for the job and that he might weigh the possibility of hiring me anyway and just training me on the machine, but that might not be "cost advantageous." After all, he was a one-man firm and he had a lot to consider. My eyes just glistened and tears started to roll all over the Dictaphone machine. I just wanted a big hole to open up and suck me in. Then he saw the tears and he felt awful and he tried to make it better but it just got worse. I stood up and ran out of there. His office was on the second story inside a building. I ran out the door and down the stairs. He yelled after me to come back and that he was sorry. I just kept running down those stairs. I think I skipped a few stairs. I yelled that I was sorry, but I just had to go, and thank you again. I yelled all that while running down thirty stairs, crying, and waving my left hand. I got in my car and I just cried. I still had to find my way back to the freeway and figure out where the heck I was.

WHAT? ~

What on earth am I doing here?

I was fine for a moment, now great! Here come

Some tears.

Calm down, concentrate

Get a grip

Say a prayer, take a breath

Here's some water

Take a sip.

What am I doing?

I thought I was fine

My confidence, my faith?

Where'd it go?

I'm in a bind.

Lord, I just knew

I was doing the right thing

Before all this happened

And the chaos bells started to ring.

Now here I am,

Lord, the time for the rapture

Would be now:

Please, Lord, just resume your position

Center stage

And take your bow.

I HAVE TOLD YOU THESE THINGS, so that in me you may have peace. In this world you will have trouble. But take heart! I have overcome the world!

JOHN 16:33

So DO NOT FEAR, FOR I AM WITH YOU; do not be dismayed, for I am your God. I will strengthen you and help you; I will uphold you with my righteous right hand.

ISAIAH 41:10

CHAPTER THIRTY-TWO

BROKE

I felt defeated the morning that I realized that I had $2.36 in the bank account. Nothing was going right with the finances and my husband was busy with school and out of work. I was exhausted from work, children, and the miracles I had been trying to pull off with the finances. I just wanted to cry. I guess the only good thing about having $2.36 in your bank account is that at least it's not a negative $2.36. The other good thing about that is you just get to sit back and pray, listen for God's direction and given opportunities, and then just watch God provide your needs. A friend gave me $20, my husband got paid $200 for unused sick days for the year, my grandmom extended the due date of my loan, my mom bought Jacob's baby food and cereal, my mom gave me $40, Brian got two side jobs plumbing and made $450, and I got a Christmas bonus of $500 within a week and a half of the day I realized I only had $2.36. Now, if those aren't a bunch of God's miracles, I don't know what they are! It's hard to imagine a light at the end of the tunnel when you are sitting in the dark with $2.36, but it's important to realize that God is in control. You cannot please God without faith. Therefore, I just pray that my cup runneth over and that my faith is a living example and a testimony of God's faithfulness. Praise God for his faithfulness!

BROKE ∾

I'm broke

I'm down

I'm exhausted

I'm tired

God, my faith

Seems to have lost its

Fire.

My hope

Is there, yet I wonder

How much remains

I feel so low

I have nothing to lose any more

And all to gain . . .

Your

Name

I

Called.

You

Listened

You

Heard.

I'm back

I'm strong

Thank you, Lord, for your kind words
Please help me to remember
That when I'm broke
And broken down
You are the one
Who's in control
And wears the crown.

A<small>ND SURELY I AM WITH YOU ALWAYS,</small>
to the very end of the age.

MATTHEW 28:20

CHAPTER THIRTY-THREE

MY OFFERING

It happens to be a Tuesday night. Tomorrow is Wednesday and the children and I will be going to church. Faith was talking about wearing the new dress my good friend bought her. This dress has a purse that matches. It may as well be called a "tithing purse" because this purse is large enough to hold two quarters at the most and it's really just a fashion statement that matches the design of the dress. I told Faith that it would be perfect for her "Jesus money." She said she did not want to give any of *her* money to Jesus. I explained to her that Jesus did not want much. If she has ten pennies, then he only wants one penny. "One penny isn't much, Faith, and it's all Jesus' anyway. He just shares with us so we need to share as well." I could see her thinking quietly with her eyes looking to the upper left and her lip slightly curled, her left leg slightly bent inward and her right shoulder trying to position itself in the same slanting position that her eyes had found. "Well, I don't want to give Jesus *real* money, I'll give him some of my fake money instead." She was, of course, referring to her *Monopoly* money. I tried not to laugh and I was shocked that at four years old a child who barely knew the difference between a penny and a hundred-dollar bill could differentiate between real money and fake money. At four years old she wanted to keep all her money to herself. "Gosh," I thought to myself, "I really need to teach my child the obedient lesson of tithing and I better hurry before she turns into an earthly thief of a bank as well as an eternal thief of God. "Faith, Jesus doesn't want much at all, he only wants one penny." I really hoped repeating the same words I had just said would help because I did not have a clue as to what to say next. "Okay," she said. "I'll give Jesus one penny and I'll put it in my purse for church." She went through all her change and picked out two quarters and two pennies. Wow, she had *four* things instead of just one. She was more generous than I gave her credit for. By the time she finished rationalizing, she had put all but one penny back in her piggy bank stash. "I'll give this *one* to Jesus," she said. Well, I won't get into that whole 'tenth' lesson right now. I'm just glad she is giving. Faith hung her church purse on the handle of her dresser. Her purse and her Jesus penny would hang there until it was time to go to church.

I have a big job on my hands. Learning about tithing and teaching tithing is just a huge, continual job that I can't afford to not teach my children.

I recently listened to a tape of Jerry Falwell which changed my life and which made the whole paragraph before this one transpire. He was preaching about the responsibility of a Christian to tithe. Previous to hearing this tape I thought that surely God did not expect me to give anything because I had nothing to give. Money was always tight and I was always trying to make miracles happen with the finances. Well, if you look at the two sentences before this one you'll notice something. The word "I" is in it a bunch. Of course, God doesn't expect me to give what I don't have. He just expects me to give a little of what I have. If I have ten dollars, well then, he only wants one dollar. I was acting as if God told me to sell everything I had and give him the money. The Bible says that God only wants the first 10 percent. Looking back at the other sentence, I can't believe that I even said that "I" was trying to make miracles happen with the finances! I'm not God and I couldn't make miracles happen in any instance. Now, I can be one of God's fishers of men and make miracles happen with him, but little old me cannot make miracles happen in my finances all by myself. I decided it's about time that I gave it to God. If you've never heard of Jerry Falwell I recommend that you listen to him and request one of his tapes regarding God's commandment to tithe. I believe that it will change your life.

I had recently joined a church and I was excited about this new commitment of obedience I had made. I would go to church every Sunday regardless of how much homework I had, regardless of how many kid difficulties I encountered each Sunday morning, and regardless of how many chores I had to do around the house. Because you know what? All those things I just mentioned will never go away. My homework may go away, but by that time my children will be bringing their homework home. So all the above-mentioned chores are just a part of everyday life and they really aren't good enough excuses for not attending church or for not tithing. I have avoided making a commitment to a church for years now. I told my mom today that making the commitment to go to church seems as difficult a commitment to keep as someone who is trying to quit smoking. I'm sure if my pastor, Dr. Merritt, is reading this he's thinking that I could have come up with a better analogy. It is hard for me, though. I was not raised in the church but I want my children to be raised in the church. It is part of my responsibility as a Christian parent to show my children a Christian lifestyle. I have to make commitments and keep them if I am to teach them about the ultimate commitment, God's commitment to us.

So, today is Sunday. My husband works every weekend. He's a Senior in college and he is presently student teaching. He is so busy with grading papers and making lesson plans and teaching during the week that he reserves the weekend to work side plumbing jobs. So, it's just me and the kids and a commitment I made to God, to myself, and to my kids to go to church every Sunday. The first Sunday we went was about a month ago. It was pouring down rain, I forgot the umbrella, and the only parking spot left was a mile from the front door, so that gives you an idea of what we looked like by the time we reached the front steps of the church. There was a man standing there, apparently waiting for whoever was fetching the car. Anyway, he took one look at me and said, "It's a big job today, isn't it?" "Yes," I said, as I prepared to shake my head like a dog coming inside from a frolic in the rainy woods. I thought to myself, "*Today*? It's a big job any day, and by myself for that matter." "I can do this," I told myself, "I can do this." Like a smoker who says, "I've been nicotine free for one month now," I was the new churchgoer who could say, "I've been going to church for four Sundays straight and I'm not giving in to the same ol' lifestyle of selfish Sundays that I used to live." Yep, I've been going strong for four whole weeks and darn proud of it. It's hard, though. Getting two children to church by myself was as huge of an accomplishment as a chain-smoker giving up cigarettes. I really had to go to church now that I had made a commitment to tithe as well. (Boy, I was just full of commitments lately.)

When I made my decision to tithe I was sitting at work and a wonderful Christian friend had made the same decision as well. In fact, it was this good friend who had loaned me the tape and who had witnessed to me about the work God was waiting to do in the lives of his people if they (we) would just trust in him to be in control of everything. That "everything" included money. How could I expect God to work in my finances if I wasn't even giving him one dollar? The Bible says (and I'm paraphrasing), "He who he trusts with little he will trust with much." Well, if I was the manager of a bank and I had an employee who couldn't balance accounts and who was constantly miscrediting accounts, I sure would not ask him to balance the corporate account nor would I keep him as part of the staff. Why then would or should God trust me with managing more of his money when I had done a hideous job with the little he did allow me to have?

We had $66.65 in our checking account (we had a savings account "concept" opened but there was never real money in it) when I decided to give 10 percent. I'd have to wait for the next pay period to give 10 percent of my paycheck, but for now, for this Sunday, I'd give 10 percent of what I have at this very moment. Six dollars is what I'd give this coming Sunday. It doesn't seem like much, but to me it was the equivalent of what

$1,000 is to others. Of course, by the time Sunday rolled around I had to buy more formula for Jacob and more fruit for Faith. I spent $47 at the store that night on things we really needed, food. I drove home praying to God about how I was just going to trust in him and I was giving $6 this coming Sunday even if it meant I would have to get $6 worth of quarters from the quarter can in the garage. I was also praying about the fact that I needed a new car seat for Jacob (great, another $60 or so) and I did not have the money for one. I knew Brian would work this weekend, but there was no telling how much he would make. Hopefully he would make $100 but even if he did make $100 we would need that for more food until I got paid in another week and a half. At this point I said out loud, "God, we only have $19.65 to our name. I cannot even begin to think about all the work that needs to be done on my teeth. If they all rot out, then so be it. If that's the case then please help me pay for dentures. I'm twenty-five years old and I feel so old and I'm so tired. We're broke, dear God, so broke. But I am giving $6 this Sunday because its 10 percent of what I had when I made the decision to tithe. I just give it to you, dear God, I just give it to you." By this time I was home. I pulled up in the driveway next to my mom's car. "Huh," I thought to myself, "what is she doing here at 8:00 at night? Maybe she forgot to bring her vacuum home today." (Ours was broken and we had borrowed hers.) She and her husband were standing in our living room with bags of goodies everywhere! They had bought a new car seat for Jacob, a new outfit for Jacob, two cans of formula for Jacob, a whole cupboard of baby food for Jacob, three new outfits for Faith, a bag of apples . . . I just about fell over! I had not even tithed yet! I had simply made the commitment to tithe and look what God did! The extraordinary thing is that my mom is probably just as broke or more broke than I, but somehow she and her husband had done all this. It was truly amazing.

God is so faithful to his children! I want to teach my children faith like that. I need to commit to a church and commit to tithing to do that. So, back to this Sunday. It was the big day. I had my $6 in change in the side pocket of the diaper bag and I was so excited to go to church and to give it to God. The service started at 11:00. With two young children, 11:00 is practically dinnertime at my house when you consider how long everyone has already been up by the time the little hand is on the 11 and the big hand rests on the 12! Church at 11 equals easy as pie. I think *not*. Jacob was bathed, dressed, bag packed and ready (check). I was ready. I had my makeup on, my hair done, my panty hose on, my church blouse on, my coat to my suit next to the diaper bag, my skirt next to the diaper bag ready to put on right before I went out the door. I never put my skirt on before kids were loaded because if I did I knew I'd slit the slit five miles upward picking, pulling, loading, stretching, running, etc. in my efforts to get everyone else ready. So, I was ready (check). Faith had eaten, brushed her hair and teeth, and all she needed was to get dressed. Well, she starting throwing a fit about what I had picked for her to wear. In the middle of her fit Jacob decided he wanted a bottle. So I fed him. Okay, it is now 10:45. Church is only four miles down the road. We may make it before the service ends. All I had to do was get Faith dressed. Faith, of course, wanted to wear her stretch pants with the paint on them from when she helped me paint the bathroom and a stained T-shirt and her tennis shoes. We only had $6 to give, but I didn't want the church to think we lived in a box so I pleaded with Faith to wear this, or this, or this, or that. To no avail. I finally said, "We are *not* going to church!" Well, if you think Faith was crying before I said that, she really starting crying after I said that.

"I want to go to church, I want to see my friends, I want to see Jesus, I want to see the puppets," she said in between sobs and blowing her nose all over her shirt. I felt the Holy Spirit come to me. I wanted to ask the Holy Spirit to transform into human form and help me get Faith dressed, the car loaded, the kids to church, and it would also be a nice touch if Jesus would escort me to a pew in the worship center. Kinda like the way Samantha on *Bewitched* used to do when she wiggled her nose. "Wiggle wiggle" and the room was cleaned, or dinner was made, or whatever silly things Samantha used to do. Instead, though, the Holy Spirit gave me peace. Peace in the midst of turmoil or trouble is an amazing thing! I calmed down. I got a grip and I told Faith that next Sunday we would pick out her church clothes the night before so that all she would have to do is get dressed all by herself in whatever she had picked out the night before. How genius! Let the child think she will be in control then she'll really be excited about getting dressed in the outfit *she* chose and prepared the night before. Wow, God: You are so smart! Faith and I compromised. She wore a slightly fancy T-shirt instead of the stained one. She picked different stretch pants and I did let her wear her tennis shoes. "Heck," I thought to myself, "I don't think God will mind if Faith shows up *not* looking like Shirley Temple with black patent leather shoes on and some frilly dress with a fancy button-down coat and a church hat on. I think God will just be glad that she is there. He may even command one hundred angels to sing in heaven upon our arrival at church because it will be such a miracle in itself that we even made it!

We got to the church at 11:20! Wow, at least forty more minutes left in the service. We dropped Jacob off (check). I took Faith to her room and miraculously enough, she did not even tear my leg off or scream when I left the room (check). I went to the Worship Center. As I walked down the hall toward the doors I felt like it was already midnight. I had already experienced a full day and it had only just begun. I knew I was hideously late but I found one of the only seats that wasn't taken yet (practically hidden behind some flowers and a wall about four feet under the pulpit) and I sat down. Who cares. I was just glad to sit and I came for the purpose of giving my tithe! Well, the sermon was awesome. I laughed and cried and praised God and I had so much fun. I practically forgot about the mountain the Holy Spirit and I had moved just to get here. It came time to tithe. "Oh no!" I had left my quarters in Jacob's diaper bag! Now what? I decided to slip out and get the kids and get back before the offering was over. By the time we made it back everyone was gone. I and my two children, a diaper bag, my big Bible, and my quarters walked all over the place trying to find the preacher so we could give $6. I couldn't find the preacher, I couldn't find anyone! Everyone was bustling around trying to leave, cleaning up, and finding their own children. The kids and I just sat down on a bench in some hallway. I still get lost around the church. One lady who I recognized as a greeter, or a Sunday school leader, asked if she could help me. I guess I looked lost. I told her I was just looking for the preacher because I forgot my tithe money in my son's diaper bag and by the time I got my children and the money the service was over and the preacher was nowhere to be found. Another lady came up by this time and she said that if I had an envelope or something I could put my money in there and she would turn it in. I didn't have an envelope and this lady was gonna crack up when she realized I wasn't turning in a nice little check or a $50 bill. She traveled the road of Damascus and about ten minutes later she came back with an envelope for me. She told me to just write my name on it . . . that would be a problem since I did not have pen . . . and she would turn it in. I told both ladies that I only had $6 in *change* and that I didn't want credit for it, but that I just wanted to turn it in, and thanks for the envelope, but I didn't have a pen to write my name on it. They didn't have a pen either and I didn't want this poor lady to have to travel the long road again in search of a pen so that I could write my name on a bumpy envelope of quarters so that I could get tax credit for my contribution. She left and brought back a pen and I wrote my name on the envelope on top of the bumpy quarters while holding Jacob, Faith's hand, and a diaper bag, and I tithed the $6 I said I was going to tithe earlier that week! Both ladies sighed when they saw me put my quarters in the envelope as I was telling them about my commitment to tithe and how this was 10 percent of what I had. They probably thought I was a single mom just like everyone else. Who knows what they thought. I know what I thought, though. I felt like I had climbed a mountain and giving that bumpy envelope of quarters to God as my first tithe was like putting a flag at the top of Mt. Everest because Jesus' blood, my sweat, and Faith and Jacob's tears went into that tithe and I was proud and thankful for the victory.

I have made the commitment to God that he has so desired since I first walked with him. I have committed myself to tithe. There are some very distinct things that God promises us when we tithe. For one, to *not* tithe is to rob God. If you have a moment, read Malachi. It's a short book but it's about how the people brought their sick sheep, their most ugly sheep to the sacrificing alter. They figured since they were going to kill them anyway, and it was only for God, why not just get the lame ones and keep the best sheep for themselves. God replies to this in Malachi 1:8 when he says, "And if ye offer the blind for sacrifice, is it not evil? And if ye offer the lame and sick, is it not evil? Offer it now unto thy governor; will he be pleased with thee, or accept thy person, saith the LORD of hosts." Most of us, including myself, are in financial bondage with bills simply because we have robbed God to begin with. Financial bondage reaches its scaly, bitter, bony fingers into the depths of other aspects of our lives until we are as spiritually bound as we are financially bound. It can happen. It happened to me and it is happening to many, many other families and people in this country. God promises us something, though. He promises us eternal life when we first meet him and then he promises us much, much more than that. God's promises to us are dependent, however, on us. I've missed a lot of God's promises (blessings) in my life the last couple years because, as we all know, I was not listening to God. I'm not here to preach fire and brimstone because this book is my testimony and my sermon to you, but I do want you to know one thing. The book of Malachi is about more than the people robbing from God, it's about his promises to us once we quit robbing him and start giving back to him. In Malachi, God says some very distinct things:

Give me a little and I'll give back more than you ever dreamed.
Give me a little and I'll protect what you have.
Give me a little and I'll give you a personal, powerful testimony to tell others of my faithfulness.
(Give me a little and I'll give back more than you ever dreamed.)

"Bring ye all the tithes into the storehouse, that there may be meat in mine house, and prove me now herewith, saith the LORD of hosts, if I will not open you the windows of heaven, and pour you out a blessing, that there shall not be room enough to receive it. (Give to me and I'll give back a hundredfold.)

(Give to me and I'll protect what you have.) "And I will rebuke the devourer for your sakes, and he shall not destroy the fruits of your ground; neither shall your vine cast her fruit before the time in the field, saith the LORD of hosts."

(Give to me and I will bless you in order that you have a personal testimony to tell others what I, your Lord, have done for you.)

BRING THE WHOLE TITHE INTO THE STORE-house, the whole tithe, that there may be food in my house. Test me, this says the LORD Almighty, and see if I will not throw open the floodgates of heaven and pour out so much blessing that you will not have room enough for it. I will prevent pests from devouring your crops, and the vines in your fields will not cast their fruit," says the LORD Almighty. Then all the nations will call you blessed, for yours will be a delightful land," says the LORD Almighty.

MALACHI 3: 10-12

I was reading Isaiah before my family was awake on the first Sunday that I tithed 10 percent of my gross. I decided to prepare my envelope and write a Bible verse on it as well as my greatest need at the time. I wrote, "Lo, everyone that thirsteth, come ye to the waters, and he that hath no money; come ye, buy, and eat; yea, come, buy wine and milk without money and without price" Isaiah 55:1. I also wrote, "So that I may buy baby formula without money." I felt so excited as I put my first tithe of 10 percent in the offering plate. I felt as if I were placing it in the hands of God. I was, really. I give it to the church because the church is the storehouse, but I am really giving it to God. What an honor! In Philippians 4:18 it says, "But I have all and abound: I am full having received of Epaphroditus the things which were sent from you, an odour of a sweet smell, a sacrifice acceptable, well pleasing to God." My tithe has a sweet scent when it is received in heaven! That is amazing! God is amazing!

That was about ten weeks ago, and can I tell you something truly amazing? I have not had to buy baby formula since I wrote down that verse and my need! My mother and her husband have continually supplied baby formula and I never even asked them! I never even told anyone I was tithing or what I was doing! They stop by and knock on the door and walk in with baby formula (and diapers, and baby food) or they leave it in my car and I find it the next morning! I'll tell you something; You can't out-give God! One blessing after another has happened in regard to my household finances. They are so bountiful that I can't begin to write down all of them. I'm keeping a journal, though, of all the blessings that God has poured forth since I made the commitment to tithe.

Was it hard to make such a commitment especially when we were so broke to begin with? Was it hard to only pay half of my car gas bill, instead of the whole thing, for the first time in eight years because I had made this decision to tithe? Of course it was! When you call something your own (it's *my* money) for so long it seems impossible to let go of it. I was running ahead of God like a child who darts past her parent and races to the playground. The obedient act of tithing puts me back next to God, holding his hand, and looking up to him for direction. Tithing keeps one's finances in line, one's actions in line, and one's heart in line. Once all this is in order, God is free to bless his children as he has promised. He's free to reign over the money, the individual life, and the day. As I told Faith, "It's all his anyway; he's just sharing with us, so we have to share with him."

I'm calling on God to pour out these blessings that he talks about in the Bible. I don't just wait for financial freedom, I wait for spiritual blessings in the lives of my children, in my husband, in my marriage, in my brothers, in my enemies. I'm looking for all of it! I am like a bird-watcher who patiently watches a tree all day in hopes of that one special red cardinal. I am a child of God who knows of his love and that counts on him to keep his promises. God does not lie.

P.S. A couple of weeks have passed since I wrote this particular story. I have an update for you:

I do not know why I wrote about "the bird-watcher," besides, of course, the obvious, that it is a good description of how a child of God looks upward to the sky, toward him, in search of his blessings. I just write what feels right at the time. Sometimes I surprise myself when I write. Well, it was 7:00 A.M. on a Sunday morning. I had gotten up early and I ran up to the gas station to get a Sunday paper. I love to get up early and read the paper and drink coffee, and go running before the kids get up and before the Sunday morning routine of getting ready for church gets started. I went to the change drawer to get some change and it was empty! I spent fifteen minutes searching the couch cushions, junk drawers, my jewelry box, and any other place I could think of looking for $2 in change so that I could buy a paper. I wanted to cry because we were so broke. I finally found enough money in change and I dashed out of the house to get the paper. On my way to and from the gas station I just talked with God. "God, you've got to have more for us than this. I'm one of your children, and I'm trying to be so obedient and tithe, and raise my kids your way. When are things going to turn around?" I think I had a few tears roll down my checks as I pulled into the driveway at 7:10 that Sunday morning, when guess what I saw? A red cardinal! He was beautiful! He was the brightest red you have ever seen. He flew down and landed right in front of our pink-blossoming cherry tree in the front yard. I have never seen such a beautiful sight. "My red cardinal!

Thank you God. That red cardinal will carry my faith this week!" I spoke out loud as I said those words because I was so excited about God's faithfulness.

God had taken the words I had written weeks earlier and he flew them in front of me in the form of a beautiful red cardinal. God is faithful. We may not always understand how he operates, but we can rest in the assurance that he is all-knowing and all-loving.

Later that year God placed a red cardinal family in a nest in the azalea bush next to our front porch!

MY OFFERING ∾

My offering today

Is small in the eyes of man

But, Lord, I know you'll appreciate it

And my heart you understand.

Lord, today I offer

A tithe unto your plan

That it may be used to help others

Here, I place it in your hand.

I will no longer claim

Anything as my own

For God, it's yours to begin with

This lesson tithing

To me has shown.

Today it is just silver quarters

But in your eyes I know it's gold

As I place it in your hand, it's your hand
That I hold.

AND MY GOD WILL MEET ALL YOUR NEEDS
according to his glorious riches in Christ Jesus.

PHILIPPIANS 4:19

GIVE AND IT WILL BE GIVEN TO YOU. A good
measure, pressed down, shaken together and
running over, will be poured out into your lap.
For with the measure you use, it will be
measured to you.

LUKE 6:38

CHAPTER THIRTY-FOUR

CREATE IN ME

I have an exciting idea for a series of "feel-good" products. I want to put my idea on coffee mugs, stationery, shirts, calendars, and sticky notes. I want my idea to be everywhere for everyone. I want my message of God's love to reach people in a larger spectrum than Hallmark cards reach people. I had some money set aside to get my idea printed and packaged on stationery, but life seemed to have absorbed the money. I needed a root canal, Brian hit a deer with the car, and groceries and bills seemed to take priority. I wracked my mind trying to figure out how to do it all. After a few weeks I was praying on the way home and I asked God to forgive me for trying to conquer the world in one day. My ideas, my drawings, my poetry, my creativity is not mine as much as it is God's. "I'll let you handle all the logistics, Lord, after all, you are in control of all things and you do have a perfect plan." I'm going to continue to dream big, but for now on I'm going to let God handle the "big" part.

CREATE IN ME 〜

Create in me a wondrous work

Of beautiful art and form

Create in me a heart

Full of your love

That's warm.

Create in me a product

Of such glorious light

That others when they see it

Will be convinced of your might.

Create in me a spirit

Of peace and hope and joy

Create in me a love

That you sent within your

Little boy.

Create in me, oh Lord,

A soul of grace and beauty

Create in me your artwork

So that all can

See.

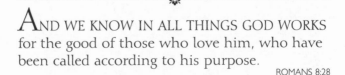

AND WE KNOW IN ALL THINGS GOD WORKS
for the good of those who love him, who have
been called according to his purpose.

ROMANS 8:28

CHAPTER THIRTY-FIVE

DREAM BIG

I am reminded of a poem I wrote in the middle of this book. It's called "In the Middle." I'm sure it rings a bell for you. I'm amazed at God's direction in my life. My cousin called me Lilith one day. Do you remember Lilith from the TV series *Cheers*? If you don't, she was the real rigid wife of Frazier Crane who hardly ever cracked a smile, who was always serious, and she always had her day, her life, and her outfit planned to a "T." My cousin asked me to do something one day and I did not think I could work it into my schedule. My cousin commented, "What's the matter, Lilith, if it's not written on your planner you just can't do it?" I've chuckled about that numerous times because I've always been the type to plan things out, to write them down, and then to check them off when I have completed them. Sometimes the truth hurts. Sometimes the truth is hilarious.

I'm going to tell you the relevance of this story now and you will be amazed, but more importantly you will be reminded of God's mysterious, but perfect, ways. I never dreamed in a million years that when I started writing a book about the struggle of going to college full-time, working full-time, and raising my daughter, that my book would evolve into a much larger story and cover a wider spectrum of everyday struggles. I never imagined that my book would have stories and poetry about my new son whom God named Jacob for me! I never imagined that God had something planned for me other than what I had perfectly planned for myself.

I grew up on welfare. I have one uncle who went to college. He served in Vietnam and in Saudi Arabia. He's college educated and he's an outstanding man. He's the only one other than my older brother who has a college degree in my whole family. In fact, I can say that at least 90 percent of my extended family is plagued with the disease of alcoholism. It's a crying shame. I decided at a young age that I would not be an alcoholic and that I would be extremely educated. I planned my life so completely that I had an imaginary mountain in my mind that I was climbing. I had placed so many flags of accomplishment along my trail up that mountain that I was proud of the miles I had thus far climbed. I was checking each moment of success off my Lilith list and I was almost at the top of my mountain. I was almost ready to place the largest flag, college graduation, on top of my mountain when I became pregnant with Jacob.

For a brief moment I tumbled down the side of my mountain. I tumbled and scratched my pride on bushes. I think I even broke a part of my pride as I landed with a thud at the bottom of a pit. I was stuck there for a while as I tried to figure out how I had gotten there. I tried to regain consciousness and figure out where I was. Guess what happened as I lay broken in this pit which existed on the side of my mountain? God taught me something very important. God told me that he had a plan for me that was greater than my plan for myself. God taught me that I could not always have what I wanted when I wanted it. God told me that I was going to have a son and name him Jacob in 1998. He told me that I would not graduate from college in 1998, but that his plan was more perfect than mine. I will not sit here and tell you that I wasn't devastated. I was. I had to accept that my childhood dream of college and success would not happen in 1998. I had to accept that a degree in college did not spell success. Real success is found in a close personal relationship with Jesus Christ. Jacob is six months old now. God has been working on me in this area since October of 1997 when he first whispered the name Jacob in my ear. I've been a stubborn child. I've acted childish as I struggled to hold on to my dreams instead of God's will in my life. I've climbed out of the pit, though. I've come a long way. Against my own desires, I've decided to wait until Brian graduates from college before I return to college full-time. I've realized that although I've wanted my college degree so bad that I could just taste it, God has even sweeter things for me for now. I can have my dream of college and success, but I must seek his kingdom first and then all these things will be added unto me.

DREAM BIG ∼

Dream big,

Says the Lord,

For it's the desires of your heart that I have for you.

Dream big

But seek me first

In all you say and all you do.

In black, white, and red

You put your word,

I said to God one day.

Help me to remember that when I seek for

Answers and act absurd.

For you it's black and white

There's no gray to figure out.

Lord, please help me

To think like you and erase
My doubt.
I will seek ye first
And not worry about the rest.
Lord, just please help me
Arise victoriously through
Every test."

YOU HAVE GRANTED HIM THE DESIRE OF HIS
heart and not withheld the request of his lips.

PSALM 21:3

CHAPTER THIRTY-SIX

THE BUGS MUST BE CONFUSED

T he bugs must be confused," I heard a friend say at work one day. She was making small cordial talk to a supply man or a service man about something she needed for the office. It was November in Georgia and we had been having unusually warm weather. "Yes, I know," she said as she continued to expand about the wonderful spring weather we were having this winter. I immediately picked up my wallet and chicken-scratched the words: "The bugs must be confused." What a perfect sentence! What perfect words to exemplify the confusion in society. "Geez," I thought to myself. "She's right. If the bugs, whose body mass makes up one or just a few cells, are confused about what's going on in the world, it's no wonder why we, multi-million-celled organisms, are confused about the world as well."

We multi-million-celled organisms have as many more issues to deal with as we have cells. Society seems to be falling in around us. Crime, disrespect, corruption in this, that, or the other, diseases on the epidemic level, improper treatment of the old, the young. Then there's the confusion we have in our own minds about who we are as individuals, as parents, as children, as friends, what we are supposed to be doing in our own lives. The huge questions hang over our heads. Is this as good as it gets? Will it always be this hard? Will I always be this tired? And by the way, What is going on with the weather? Storms in the atmosphere, storms within our minds, either way, it's pretty obvious that if the bugs are confused, so, too, are we.

The only conclusion I have to any of that is that God never said it was going to be easy, he only said that he would send us a comforter, The Holy Spirit, to comfort us. And the only other comment I have to all those thoughts that I just had to throw out into the space of your mind is this: "Jesus Christ is the same yesterday, today, and forever." And so, as we deal with this crazy weather, whether that storm resides in the clouds or in the clouds of our mind, we must remember that though the world changes and although the world is full of uncertainty, God does *not* change like the weather and you can be sure that his love surpasses any warmth one might feel on a summer day.

THE BUGS MUST BE CONFUSED ~

The bugs must be confused

Well, yeah, so am I

One moment I'm in a cocoon

The next I'm told to fly.

The bugs must be confused

Such as ants on a hill

Don't you think that they wonder

When they can quit marching and just be still?

Caterpillars, geez, don't ya think they get hot
In all that fur, and don't ya think some are confused
as to where they should be
Since some end up as squished "spots"?
Beetles, what's their story?
They just seem to fly around
Looking aimlessly for
Some ground.
Bugs are just bugs and all we know
Is they crawl, they fly, they die.
I'm so glad that although I'm one of his many
little children,
God hears me when I sigh.

❖

YOU, DEAR CHILDREN, ARE FROM GOD AND
have overcome them, because the one who
is in you is greater than the one who is in
the world.

1 JOHN 4:4

CHAPTER THIRTY-SEVEN

IN THE EYES OF HEAVEN

A good friend and I have been laughing and talking about the day I finish my book. We've had a lot of fun discussing what type of outfit I will wear when Oprah asks me to be a guest on her show. We've discussed whether I should wear my red suit, my dark blue suit with the gold buttons, or just go out and buy a new one. After all, it is for the Oprah Show! As you can see I'm quite the comedian and quite the dreamer when it comes to my goals.

I was praying the other day about my book. I asked God to use it for his good. If I never end up on the Oprah Show, then so be it. If my book somehow leads just one person to Christ then it will have served its purpose. My book may never bring fame and fortune to my life, but because it gives glory to God it is already a "best-seller" in the eyes of heaven.

IN THE EYES OF HEAVEN ∾

In the eyes of heaven
I will seek for success
In the eyes of heaven
I will try to do my best.
In the eyes of heaven
I will be found
Spreading God's great love.
In the eyes of heaven
My life will reflect
Light from above.

❖

WHEN A MAN'S WAYS ARE PLEASING TO THE
LORD, he makes even his enemies live at peace
with him.

PROVERBS 16:7

CHAPTER THIRTY-EIGHT

"Look God, No Hands!"

I was drinking a cup of coffee the other day when an image flashed through my mind. Suddenly, I was ten years old again. I was riding bikes with my friend Marcie. We had ridden our bikes up to our elementary school, played on the bars as if we were Olympic gymnasts, raced toward home, kept our lives as we passed the two houses with the vicious dogs, and now we were descending a huge, long hill. She was ahead of me and I could see her blonde hair blowing behind her. I caught a quiet scent of the skunk cabbage as we passed the creek by her house. It was the end of spring, lawn mowers hummed in the background, the Saturday mailman was long behind us at Marcie's neighbors' house. She put her hands up in the air and I decided to do the same. Her dad was in the front yard working when we passed and she yelled, "Look, Dad, no hands!" We were brave. We were free. We were ten.

This image usually comes and goes throughout my mind at various times. Each time I sing and raise my hands toward the Lord this image pops up. I sit in bumper-to-bumper traffic numerous times throughout the work-week. I take advantage of this time to pray and to sing to God. When traffic is at a stand-still I sing and raise both hands toward the Lord. I feel like saying, "Look, Dad, no hands!" After all, I never had an earthly father but I've always had a heavenly Father. And so I sing and raise my hands to the Lord. The words, "Look, Dad, no hands" have come to mean a lot more in my adult life. I was once a brave ten-year-old quickly gliding down a hill on my bike with my hands raised to the sky. I am now a brave adult who still raises my hands to the sky, but for different reasons. I'm a brave woman struggling with life's battles, but I'm wise enough to know that I have to take my hands off the steering wheel of my life and let God do the driving. "Look, Father, no hands" means I've traded my ten-year-old heart of bravery for an adult heart full of God's love, seeking his wisdom.

I was telling this to a friend and I commented on what the people in other cars must think when they look across silent car windows at a woman with her arms raised toward the sky and her lips moving like she is in a professional lip-synch contest. My friend just smiled and said she did it all the time too and what a witness it is for those who see us do it. She said she can't wait for the summer day when windows are rolled down and she's sitting in traffic praising God. As soon as someone looks at her like she is odd she is just going to say, "Well, I'd hate for the rocks to have to cry out." If we do not praise and sing to God then the rocks will. I'm going to make sure the rocks keep their jobs as rocks and I keep my end of the bargain as one of God's children.

"LOOK GOD, NO HANDS!" ~

I'm going through my life with

All its plateaus and hills

As someone who praises God

And tries to do his will

I've taken my hands off the steering wheel

To look to God for direction

Because the map I seem to have charted

Is full of imperfection.

I sing and praise his name

Because there is no other

who can help me

Be a good child, wife,

and mother.

I lift his name on high as I raise my hands to him

As a ten-year-old child rides her bike and says,

"Look, Dad, no hands, look what I can do."

YOU WILL GO OUT IN JOY AND BE LED FORTH
in peace; the mountains and hills will burst
into song before you, and all the trees of the
field will clap their hands.

ISAIAH 55:12

CHAPTER THIRTY-NINE

MY LIFE

I love movies like *Sleepless in Seattle, While You Were Sleeping, Hope Floats, How to Make an American Quilt, Breakfast at Tiffany's, Pillow Talk, As Good As It Gets,* and *You've Got Mail.* I love all these movies because they are about life. They are romantic comedies that leave the audience with a warm fuzzy, and that is exactly what I like about them. These movies are about characters with lives just like everyone else. Characters in these movies are alone, heartbroken, trying to make something of their lives setting goals and achieving them through college or hard work, they are about the human battle of realizing true feelings, true pain, and understanding the depths of their souls. They are about finding out who they are, with or without someone else. Most of these movies have attracted people in flocks for one important reason: These movies are about characters to whom most of us can relate. These characters remind us of ourselves. These stories remind us of our own stories. We all laugh the hardest at movies when we see parts of ourselves in the characters. Besides, it's much more pleasant to cry and laugh about someone rather than our selves.

I'd love to turn my life into a movie, so that I can go watch it and escape from it at the same time. My life as a movie would be funny, touching, full of victorious battles, and it would end with a warm fuzzy about the true meaning of life. Writing it would be a challenge. I guess I'm writing the story of my life every day that I live. My story won't be over until my life is over so I guess I'll just keep living and keep writing.

I've said and heard some great one-liners that I know would be perfect for the big screen. The audience would laugh, cry, and relate to these one-liners just as I have done with so many great one-liners I've heard in the movies. My life may never turn into a box hit like *Sleepless in Seattle* or *You've Got Mail*. My life may never touch as many lives as it would if it made it to the big screen, but my life is still its own movie. Others watch me every day. My children watch my actions, my coworkers notice my goals. My peers in my classes watch me as I comment and learn about literature. My audience is all around me and I need to make sure that I set an example and leave as many people as possible with warm fuzzies. My life story may never be told in Hollywood or on the big screen, but my life story will be told by the memories I make and the people I touch.

MY LIFE ∿

What pressure there is

To write a poem called "My Life."

I need to make sure I speak with wisdom

And get the plot just right.

What an honor there is

In living each day and so I try to

Touch positively those who pass my way.

My life, my life, may the people

Watch and learn from me

May God's glory be seen

Victoriously.

My life be a movie in itself

May it always be remembered and watched

Like a favorite movie up on the shelf.

May my life teach and inspire

Others to run far from Satan's

Fire.

May my life make people stand

And cheer

Like a movie voted

Best for the year.

May my life make heaven sing,

And may my life echo

Like the sweet hum of a choir's

Ring.

A FTER THIS I LOOKED, AND THERE BEFORE me was a door standing open in heaven. And the voice I had first heard speaking to me like a trumpet said, Come up here, and I will show you what must take place after this.

REVELATION 4:1

CHAPTER FORTY

GOD AND COFFEE, IN THAT ORDER

That bad stand-up comedian is back. I can't seem to avoid the bad comedian act because my life just keeps asking for her to come back on stage. A funny thing happened to me on my way to *finishing* this book. Once upon a time a college degree meant more to me than sleep, it meant more to me than Saturdays with my child, it meant more to me than quality time with my husband, it meant more to me than life. I want a college degree so passionately that I will kiss my diploma once I finally earn it, but I realized something. It's not worth losing my kids, my husband, and my life in pursuit of it. I will say again, though, I want it, I want it, I want it, I want it! There, I figure I've acted like a spoiled child constantly ignoring God's command, so why not throw a small tantrum on paper real "quick like" just to make sure that we all know I've acted like a brat. I started writing this book because I used to tell everyone . . . "How do I do it all? Oh, that's an easy one, God and coffee, in THAT order." The thing about putting "God" in a sentence and using it all the time, and the thing about asking God into your life, instead of just in your sentences, well, the thing is, if you ask him to be there, he will. And if you ask God to do his will in your life, he will. So be ready, my friends, and be willing to accept his will and don't do what I've done and rationalize what he says into something you want to hear.

I've rationalized God's will so much that if "The Rationale of God's Will 101" would have ever been a class, I would have aced that class too. Most real good, earth-shattering, heart-stopping, tear-jerking books have a unique twist at the end of them that just make the reader say, "Wow, I never expected that!" This book is not different from any of those. I'm the writer and even I'm surprised. God has been writing this book through me, though, and since he is the real author I can say, "Wow, I never expected that!" I never expected that a book about the strength of God and the goal of a college degree would end the way it is ending. I never imagined that the strength I've received from God is the strength to *not* graduate right now. I never imagined that the strength I would receive from God would be the strength to do his will instead of my own. I never knew that *God and Coffee, In That Order* would really be a lesson to me about the order of my life and the fact that although I said I put God first, I really never did. And I never knew in a million years that I would find myself on my knees crying, praying, and asking God to forgive me for being so selfish about what I wanted for myself, a college degree.

The end of my book is almost longer than the rest of the book put together, but I'll try to say it in a nutshell. (There's that comedian again. We all know I'm long-winded and even if the nutshell was the size of a prize-winning watermelon, it wouldn't be enough room for me to wrap something up.) Jacob is eight months old. Faith will be four March 26, 1999. Brian is a senior at North Georgia College. He's student teaching and studying to take his second teaching certification test. I'm working full-time at a demanding job. Life is hectic. Even though I've written this book about putting God first and the important role of the mother in the household, I thought I could sneak a couple of college classes in. Hello! I guess the fact that God might as well have screamed the facts of my life into my right ear did not help me pay attention to what he was saying.

I had to learn the hard way that my role in life right now is to to be a wonderfully supportive wife to my husband and a superhero Christian mother to my two children. I thought, however, that I could rationalize my way back into college. After all, two Septembers had passed since I first heard God whisper "Jacob" into my right ear. Of course, I had refused to listen at first. I got over that and I took fewer classes and drank decaf coffee. See, I had obeyed. I carried Jacob, gave birth to Jacob, and got my family resettled with our new addition. I even handled the adjustment quite well myself. I worked all the weight off, went back to work, and kept my sanity through it all. I waited to go back to school until this fall. Heck, I figured I was a saint-and-a-half based on the fact that I had delayed school and based on the fact that I had "given birth." I thought I had sacrificed enough for God.

I got to thinking about it, though. How could I be through sacrificing for God just because I had put off college for eight months and because I had given birth? How could two small sacrifices be enough for God? The truth is, I'll never be through sacrificing for God. In Matthew 16:24 Jesus says, "If anyone would come after me, he must deny himself and take up his cross and follow me." A cross is not a lightweight little nothing you can put in your pocket and not be inconvenienced by. A huge wooden cross is something that is heavy, that carries with it a huge responsibility. It's hard to carry, it's exhausting to carry, but it's an honor that I don't want to miss out on. Jesus would have gotten off easy if he only had to do two measly little things, but he did a whole lot more. He paid the ultimate price, he sacrificed his life so that we may have eternal life. Well, then, as a child of God, and as a mother, I'll never be done sacrificing for others, but mainly, I'll never be through sacrificing for God.

However, I was so tired of *not* being in school. This whole book was about God's faithfulness and strength during my pursuit of a degree. It was about time I got back to the "degree" part. I was through sacrificing. (Let's not laugh at my big-head-edness here although it is rather hilarious at this point in my life.) I won't go into all the details, but two months into my *one* class this fall I about lost my mind. Anger started building up in me because I never had one second to myself to think, let alone to work on a paper for school or do my reading. Kids were throwing up with the flu, coughing with bronchitis, Brian was stessing out with all his school stuff, and everyone who said they would help me on the weekends with the kids so that I could do homework *was tied up*. What a joke. The bags under my eyes, the anger in my heart, and the feeling that, because I had sacrificed so much the last year, I was somehow *due* something, built up inside of me. I was a wreck.

I was talking with a good Christian friend about it all and God spoke to me. "Give to me now, and I'll give to you later," he said. I was discussing how it seemed to me that God just didn't mean for me to go to school now. As if having Jacob— (wake up) wasn't a big enough clue for me. (Hello.) Anyway, once I said those above words, I froze. I quit talking. The Holy Spirit was all around me. I had said that it seemed that God just wanted me to do something else right now, it seemed that God was just telling me "Give to me *now*, and I'll give to you later." I asked my friend if my hair was standing up because I felt like I was on Holy ground. I felt every hair on my arm, I felt every new hair under my scalp and they hadn't even grown through yet, I felt every molecule of oxygen that I was breathing and that I was about to breathe in, I felt like I might just be floating in mid-air, I felt for the ten seconds or so that went into that sentence that I was in the face of God. If this has never happened to you, I pray it does, and if it has happened to you, well, then, you know what it's like to hear God's command. It stops you in your tracks. I got up from my desk, I went in the bathroom, and I got down on my knees and I cried harder than I've ever cried in my life. I cried harder than I ever did as a child, I cried harder than I did when I found out I was pregnant with Jacob. I cried like a child who had just been disciplined. My heart felt like it had been torn out and stomped until the last beat quit beating. I cried because it hurt so bad to really let go (for now) of my dream of college, it hurt like a knife in my throat, and I cried because I had been so disobedient to God. I cried because God had to reprimand me for what I'd done and it hurt that I had let him down and that I had almost let my husband and my children down in pursuit of *my* dream. I cried out of thankfulness that God stopped me from making a terrible mistake and I was so thankful that I had finally heard God. I blew my nose at least three times just so I could keep crying, my shoulders shook, and I stayed on the floor long enough for my legs to go to sleep. Needless to say, it was exhausting. I could have lost everything I hold most dear to me. I could have lost my marriage and my kids (in a hundred different ways), I could have lost it all, so that I could have one degree *right now*.

Right now my job is to keep my family together, to teach my children about Jesus, and to help my husband graduate. Making dinner, making copies of a test or a worksheet for Brian, making grocery lists and keeping the refrigerator full, making the money to make it all happen, making puppets with Faith, making it to Faith's church activities, and making it to Sunday worship are the most important things I do make *right now*. I used to think that making an A in a class was almost all that mattered. God has taught me that this book and the last three and a half years has been about a lot more than God's strength in the midst of a college degree. I feel 99.9 percent (which is the same percentage of accuracy that the pill ensures) that God will allow me to go back to college, but it will be on his terms. Referring to the 99.9 percent is not a reference to a .1 percent possible God failure rate. God does not fail. I am simply expanding on the fact that one can never be 100 percent sure of anything they themselves have planned out. But if God is consulted and if God gives his approval, well, then that 99.9 percent can be changed to 100 percent. The only thing that anyone can be 100 percent sure of is that God is in control and that Jesus lives. If God does lead me back to college one day, I know it will be a better situation for me. Brian will be able to support me financially and emotionally, the way that I am supporting Brian right now. The kids will be older and hopefully sleeping through the night and I'll be able to concentrate on my studies, but that is farther down the road. I'm not going to go back to college until I have the same "holy goose bumps" I had all over me when I knew I had to quit college. Right now I'm looking for God's miracles in my life with great anticipation.

I realized the other day that three years ago I started answering people with the phrase, "God and Coffee, in that order." I also realized that it has been that long since I began writing this book. "Wow!" I thought to myself, "I can't believe how time flies. I need to finish this book before the kids go off to college. I really need to finish this book before Brian graduates and I go back to college. There won't be any time to work on a book while I'm finishing up my English degree. I'm going to wrap it up and send this book off to Oprah, twenty publishers, and the rest of my family.

I told Brian the other day that I was really struggling to finish the book. A full day of work, traffic, dinner, baths, and bedtime seems to wipe me out at the end of the day. Every night I plan on running to Walmart and/or working on my book, but I seem to fall asleep. I haven't just been tired lately, I've been hurting because I'm tired. My shins sometimes feel like the boxer's shins in the "Boxing" poem. Brian and I were sitting at a red light on our way back from a twelve-hour Christmas shopping spree when I commented on the struggle I'm having trying to complete my "best-seller." "I'm struggling to finish my book, Brian, but if you think about it my book is just about my struggles in life. Everyone has struggles every day. I just decided to write about mine and soften them with God and poetry." My struggles will continue all the days of my life so unless I want a book the size of a house, I better just wrap up this book, this chapter of my life, and then start fresh with a new chapter, a new book.

It's Christmas Eve today. I decided to finish my book with the miracle of Christmas. It's Jesus' birthday tomorrow. Faith and I will be baking Jesus a birthday cake today. Faith is next to me in the den working on an "art project" at her desk. Jacob is sitting in his bouncy chair talking with serious enthusiasm to his rattle. Brian is making waffles for Faith. There are a few dishes in the sink and a little laundry on the couch that needs to be folded. My comment to everyone was this: "I'm going to finish my book this morning." *"Today?"* Brian asked. "Yes, today," I replied. "All I need is an hour, not an hour at 2:00 A.M. when I'm exhausted and falling asleep at the computer, and not an hour in the morning before rushing off to work. All I need is an hour to wrap up my thoughts and finish my book. Then all the trumpets in heaven can sound off like they've been waiting to do. God has a group of angels specifically assigned to dance and sing upon the completion of my book. As soon as I type the last paragraph, the last sentence, the last word, and the last period, a joyful noise will be made in heaven. I can't keep heaven waiting any longer."

As I wish everyone a Merry Christmas and a Happy New Year, I ask you to remember my stories, my poetry, my struggles, my prayers. You have your own stories and struggles, but a common thread is intertwined amidst all our struggles. That common thread is God's love for us. God loved you enough to send his only son to save you (I John: 4:10). And as you struggle with sickness, finances, exhaustion, traffic, work, children, bath night, or lack of children and a non-bath night, as you struggle with a painful past or a painful present, please remember this: God has forgiven you so please forgive yourself. God loves you so please love yourself. And when the day gets to be too much, pour a cup of coffee, say a prayer, and remember that with God all things are possible.

Oh yeah, just one more thing. This book that you are reading never would have had the opportunity to be finished if I was still in college right now. I'd be working on a fourteen-page research paper as opposed to typing away on this book. My fourteen page research paper, my master's degree, and my doctorate degree will come, but it will come in God's time. Because "There is a time for everything, and a season for every activity under heaven: a time to be born and a time to die, a time to plant and a time to uproot, a time to kill and a time to heal, a time to tear down and a time to build, a time to weep and a time to laugh, a time to mourn and a time to dance, a time to scatter stones and a time to gather them, a time to embrace and a time to refrain, a time to search and a time to give up, a time to keep and a time to throw away, a time to tear and a time to mend, a time to be silent and a time to speak, a time to love and a time to hate, a time for war and a time for peace." Ecclesiastes 3. (and a time for a break and a cup of coffee!)

 God Bless!

Love,
Kristina Seymour

GOD AND COFFEE, IN THAT ORDER ~

"How do I do it all? you say.

"God, coffee, and in that order,"

I reply

Along my way.

I try to put God first

Instead of me

I try but it's hard

to see what heaven sees.

It's a challenge some days

I'm just worn out

So I grab a cup of coffee

And I try not to pout.

I put on some lipstick,

I fluff my hair

I try to love and laugh with care.

But some days I feel I'm drowning

In a coffee cup,

So I grab the edges and I hoist

My left leg up.

I climb out, I dangle

On the side

Being careful not to run further

The "run" I've been trying to hide.

How do I do it all?

"God and coffee, in that order,"

again my voice rings

and after that I do

"The NEXT thing."

ASCRIBE TO THE LORD, O FAMILIES OF nations, ascribe to the LORD glory and strength, ascribe to the Lord the glory due his name. Bring an offering and come before him; worship the LORD in the splendor of his holiness. Tremble before him, all the earth! The world is firmly established; it cannot be moved. Let the heavens rejoice, let the earth be glad; let them say among the nations, "The LORD reigns!" Let the sea resound, and all that is in it; let the fields be jubilant, and everything in them! Then the trees of the forest will sing, they will sing for joy before the LORD, for he comes to judge the earth. Give thanks to the LORD, for he is good; his love endures forever. Cry out, "Save us, O God our Savior; gather us and deliver us from the nations, that we may give thanks to your holy name, that we may glory in your praise." Praise be to the LORD, the God of Israel, from everlasting to everlasting. Then all the people said "Amen" and "Praise the LORD."

I CHRONICLES 16:28-36